C000258040

A+Awards 2015
Architizer

A+Awards 2015
Architizer

About Architizer and the A+Awards

Architizer is the premier online destination for design professionals to explore the world's best architecture and interiors, and discover the products and people behind them. Launched in 2009, the site has rapidly become the world's largest platform for architecture and design. Architizer publishes a must-read blog covering industry news, and honors the best architecture, spaces, and products annually with the A+Awards program.

The Categories

The A+Awards consist of three categories. The Typology Categories celebrate traditional building types. The Plus Categories recognize the link between global issues and the structures that society builds. The Product Categories acknowledge that symbiosis between products and building.

Typology - Architects do a lot of things—signage, branding, presentations, conferences—but at the core of our profession, we make buildings and spaces. The Typology Awards honor basic categories of such, including residential, office, commercial, transportation, cultural, institutional, landscape, student projects, and more

Plus - Architecture is everywhere and touches nearly every person on earth every day. The Plus Awards are designed to celebrate architecture's relevance through categories that highlight the issues confronting the world, such as sustainability, community, preservation, and many more

Product - Every architect and designer knows that it takes spectacular products and materials to make their designs a reality. Building on the tremendous success of last year's Product Awards, we're proud to present 30+ categories that speak to the design solutions that matter most to architects.

The Jury

Our jury is composed of 300+ jurors who hail from not only the world of architecture, but also product design, theater, government, technology, and real-estate development—the people who actually hire architects! The jury includes industry luminaries such as Steven Holl, Sou Fujimoto, Winy Maas, and Iwan Baan, as well as people from beyond architecture like Charles Adler, Jared Della Valle, John Edelman, and Roy Kim. A complete listing of the jury can be found on page 209.

Public Voting

Every category has a Jury Winner, but it also has a Popular Choice Winner. Our expert judges nominate five finalists within each award category, who are then presented online for professionals and design enthusiasts around the globe to vote for their favorites. The winners of the A+ Popular Choice Awards are honored alongside projects chosen by our jury.

The Trophy

Architizer has teamed up with Snarkitecture to create the A+Awards trophy. Like the A+Awards, Snarkitecture is concerned with the intersection of design and function, of theory and practice, and (most important) of architecture and society. Snarkitecture's mission to "make architecture perform the unexpected" rings loud and clear in its A+ trophy design.

The award begins its life as styrofoam, that material abhorred by environmentalists everywhere. It then goes through a variety of casting phases before ending up as a cube of cultured marble with a hairline crack along its equator. The statuette splits in half to reveal a black "+" rising from a micro landscape of contours. It's an interactive prize that's as dynamic and of-the-moment as the A+Awards program as a whole.

The Architizer A+Awards Book

This book celebrates the world's best architecture, but don't take my word for it. Every building in this book won a 2015 Architizer A+Award. These winners were chosen by an international jury of over 300 experts, and endorsed by over 200,000 public votes online.

Architecture is everywhere—nearly everyone in the world lives in a building and spends their time surrounded by architecture. The average American spends 90% of their time indoors. That is why we decided that architecture doesn't need another award program stuck in the echo chamber where architects tell other architects which architects they like. The industry needs to break out and re-engage with the public that actually uses our buildings!

Instead of celebrating a single honoree or making architecture into something rarefied and arcane, the A+Awards celebrate the diversity of the world's architecture. The entrants, from over 100 countries, run the gamut of architectural typology and form, ranging from the tallest towers to the tiniest apartments and everything in between. From a sinuous elevated bike path to a "human-sized birdhouse," the winners represent the full spectrum of architectural endeavor: There is a next-generation prefab construction method, a pop-up tower "grown" from mushrooms, conscientious renovations in China, and even a radical revitalization of the NYC waterfront.

Taken together, these 100 projects represent a snapshot of the very best architecture in 2015. Whether you find inspiration in the images here or you seek out these buildings and spaces in person—or you have the good fortune to encounter them in your daily life—we hope that these projects change the way you look at the world around you.

— Marc Kushner

Jury and Popular Choice Winners

Bermondsey Warehouse Loft London, UK

A loft apartment within a converted warehouse.

The client initially approached FORM design architecture to carry out some minor alterations to his apartment to better meet his needs. The industrial character and scale had been lost beneath raised floors, lowered ceilings, and partitions of a previous renovation.

Detailed discussions established how the client wanted to use the space, allowing for a flexible live/work environment tailored to his requirements in a warehouse loft environment.

Storage, bathroom, and utility functions are contained within a sharply detailed block in the corner of the now fully revealed loft space, with a similarly detailed linear counter block providing the cooking area.

A concealed sliding wall allows the sleeping area to be fully enclosed if required. At the other end, a counter provides a work area for the photographer owner. In between are flexible zones for dining, relaxing, and exercise.

With the exception of the unfinished pitch pine plank floor, all surfaces and fittings are finished in white. The crisp machine-made quality of the Hi-Macs blocks set them apart from the hand-made, time-weathered surface textures of the original industrial building.

Surface finishes within the blocks are dark gray. The removal of previous subdivisions allows shafts of sunlight from the windows in the south and west walls to animate the space.

Status
Built

Year
2011

Firm
FORM Design Architecture

Firm location
London, UK

Bermondsey Warehouse Loft London, UK

Ice & Snow Apartment Zhangjiakou, China

A softly lit, snowfield-inspired apartment blends in with the surrounding ski site.

The design of the apartment is inspired by a melting snowfield in spring, when nature slowly revives from winter and offers a contrast of cold and warm, white and colorful. This atmosphere is translated into architecture by hand-plastered, white shells covering the walls and the ceiling to create a seamless space.

Partially cut by wooden boxes, the white shells infuse warmth and nature into the space for relaxing, conversing, and displaying artwork. The walls are raised two inches and backlit, separating the white shells and fir wood floor.

The shells flow through the space, blending the hallway, public areas, and private rooms. The apartment features seven bedrooms, a large cloakroom and storage for the skiing equipment, several bathrooms, and a large living room in the center. The curved walls guide the guests to a spiral staircase, which leads to formal living and dining spaces upstairs with access to a large roof terrace. A network of heating pipes rests behind the plastered shells and emits warmth through the walls and throughout the apartment. The warmness, together with the handcrafted finish of the shells, provide a haptic and cozy feeling for guests.

Status
Built

Year
2013

Firm
Penda Architects

Firm location
Beijing, China

1.8 M Width House Tokyo, Japan

A house on a very small, narrow site where light shines in and fresh air flows between the floating floors.

This small and narrow site has tight boundaries and a crowded perimeter of surrounding buildings. The design attempts to reserve as much space as possible, as well as provide psychological openness for the resident.

In this project, we have considered a house as an aggregation of small spaces that expand over various floor levels. Floating floors in long and narrow spaces generate a spatial expanse. Light and fresh air from openings in the frontage and upper side of the building flows into every corner of the house, utilizing the floor difference. The natural light and air brings an openness, while rich, calm color gives a sense of depth to the space. Open shelves placed around the stairs and in the kitchen further enhance the spatial openness.

Structural design was developed by fully considering the singularity of the building shape. Columns and beams were limited to maximize the interior space. Steel-frame construction methods were employed for the narrow frontage site condition, EZ stake system, and basement structure. Exterior materials such as open piping routes can be easily maintained and are further adopted to match the uniqueness of the land shape. Natural wind, natural airflow, and utilization of circulation also contribute to the comfortable space.

Status
Built

Year
2012

Firm
YUUA Architects & Associates

Firm location
Tokyo, Japan

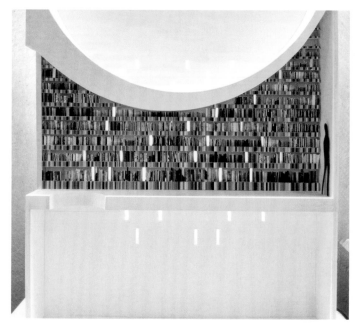

Haffenden House Syracuse, NY, USA

The project is a fabric-wrapped writing studio/guest house with a library, tub, and reading room.

The Haffenden House is a writing studio for two poets in upstate New York and includes a garage/breezeway at ground level, a library and writing space on the second level, and a curved, soft reading room on the third level. The project finds itself within the suburban realm, referencing Gianni Pettena's Ice House from 1972 as a blank spot within the repetitive image of 'house.'

The poets' studio uses a translucent, silicon-impregnated fabric skin for a light-filled writing room without any visual connection to the context on three sides. Inside the blank box between the second and third levels, the section produces a bowl-shaped division, maximizing indirect light for the second level and avoiding any association with the landscape on the third level.

Status
Built

Year
2014

Firm
PARA Project

Firm location
Brooklyn, NY, USA

Taíde House Póvoa de Lanhoso, Portugal

Taíde House is the rehabilitation of an old country house with the typical characteristics of popular architecture.

The proposal for the project stipulated that the house should dialogue with its surroundings in a friendly way, and that the design concept was not to break completely with the past. We felt that we could create something dynamic without impeding upon the surrounding environment. We understood that the surroundings work as an amphitheater in which the gaze of the neighbors, the inhabitants of those uniquely shaped roof houses, are very close. Surrounding streets are narrow, backyards are almost public, and every word is heard. The scale of the house was a concern.

In early sketches, the roof emerges, and assumes itself as the structuring element for the whole project. It organized and managed dynamic spaces in a rather simple square interior, but also allowed the compartmentalization of the exterior, creating protected areas for leisure and contemplation.

The granite walls and stairs, which involve the ancient grape mill in the ground floor, serve as a base for the whole proposal. The house is organized across two floors. The ground floor encompasses the social area, with the kitchen, bathroom, office, and a double-ceiling living room, which houses the stairwell that gives access to the upper floor with two bedrooms.

Status
Built

Year
2014

Firm
Rui Vieira Oliveira + Vasco Manuel Fernandes

Firm location
Guimarães, Portugal

Lens House London, UK

Alison Brooks Architects has extended a 19th-century house in London by adding two tapered volumes that project into the garden.

Lens House is Alison Brooks Architect's transformation of a five-story 19th-century villa in north London for a client involved in photography and design.

Conceived as a series of large apertures connected by large trapezoidal planes, these openings capture light throughout the day, draw the garden into the house, and frame precise views of the spectacular 300-year-old walnut tree.

A low single-story volume wraps around brick walls at the side of the house to create a home office and roof terrace, while the second tapered volume extends out at the back to expand the first floor living room.

Each plane of the scheme is either fully glazed or fully solid, there are no punched windows. This approach creates an architecture without mass and weight, like the folded surfaces of origami where both roof and wall planes are one material.

On the garden side, the building rests lightly on the ground with undercut walls to avoid the walnut tree's roots. Inside, the roof light geometry funnels light into the workspace throughout the day. Where the original living room once was, ABA has opened a new double-height volume. This draws south light deep into the house.

Status
Built

Year
2012

Firm
**Alison Brooks
Architects**

Firm location
London, UK

Cabin in the Woods Southampton, NY, USA

A weekend and summer house for a young family of five.

In response to the clients' desire for a modern cabin, the architect created three long cantilevers on the top of a secluded hill that gives the spaces of the house commanding views of the woods and the feeling of being suspended in the trees. The cedar-lined living and dining spaces combine to form a Great Room, with a wall of sliding glass doors looking out onto the pool and deck.

The house, for a young family of five, contains two master suites and three additional bedrooms, allowing the owners to accommodate friends with their children. The large screen porch, on one of the cantilevered ends, contains an outdoor fireplace and creates the feeling of being in a tree house. The pool's design creates the illusion of a body of water tautly suspended between two stone walls with the infinity edge beckoning to the trees beyond.

Status
Built

Year
2013

Firm
Rangr Studio

Firm location
New York, NY, USA

Casa Delta Guaruja, São Paulo, Brazil

A weekend house commissioned by a couple with three young children, located one and a half hours from São Paulo.

This weekend house is built on a sloped terrain surrounded by an important Atlantic Forest reserve in a plot allowed for building purposes. The functional program was laid out in different levels so as to let the house adapt to the existing terrain and trees in a subtle fashion.

The entrance is made from the parking spaces on the lower level, from which a wide staircase shoots up across the first floor and onto the terrace where the social areas and master suite are built under a light canopy. The first floor houses the children's suites and overhangs the stone base of the house, providing shelter to the entranceway and arriving guests. The sunscreen panels that clad this volume give privacy to the bedrooms and provide lightness and transparency to the building.

The upper floor is the most privileged part of the house, benefiting from outstanding views of the sea and beach that are less than 300 feet away. The interior and exterior grades are one and the same. The subtle canopy slope and the orientation of the timber sunscreens guide the eye towards the horizon, where an infinity edge makes the swimming pool part of the ocean.

Status
Built

Year
2014

Firm
Bernardes Arquitetura

Firm location
São Paulo, Brazil

Sambade House Penafiel, Portugal

A pure volume of raw concrete, adjusted to the ground, waits to age gracefully as time passes.

Based on the genetics of the place, the intervention's main goal is the creation of a contemporary space without disturbing the peace of the countryside area.

A pure volume with a rectangular base is adjusted to the ground and opens into the green landscape. The volumetric purity, which was desired by the client, sets the mood for the project. Further, the landscape of the place is now one of the terraced fields of the perfectly balanced ground.

The act of inhabiting unfolds through the volume of concrete: pure, raw, adjusted to the ground, and just waiting to grow old as the days go by. These thematic elements all evoke the life of the countryside.

Status
Built

Year
2014

Firm
spaceworkers

Firm location
Paredes, Porto, Portugal

Residential Complex Ciekurkrasti Baltezers, Adazi, Latvia

An accentuation of natural surroundings was at the forefront of the design process for a residential complex.

Residential complex Ciekurkrasti is located in Adazi, a suburb of Riga. It is made up of three joined blocks facing lake Baltezers to the south and frames a wide courtyard to the northwest. The residences vary from compact one-bedroom apartments to spacious 4-bedroom lofts, wide-open to their environment, and extended by vast exterior surfaces.

The plot was severely degraded during the Soviet period. It was revitalized by turning the desolate waterfront into a public beach and constructing a boating pier for the use of local residents.

Voids and openings to the landscape create terraces and tunnels. Circulation areas outside the building feature sculptural concrete stairs that rise through openings in the volume and connect the courtyard to the lower lying waterfront.

The structure is built from reinforced concrete. Parking and storage areas in the basement are connected to the levels above by lifts that open onto spacious staircases with large windows allowing natural light to enter the interior.

Each staircase has an entrance from the courtyard. The main entrance lobby is connected to the communal areas. There is a gym, a spa with a pool, and a restaurant facing the lake.

Status
Built

Year
2014

Firm
AB3D

Firm location
Riga, Latvia

Bruggerberg Brugg, Aargau, Switzerland

A multi-unit terrace house in Brugg, including 16 condominiums with individual garages.

The building defies the conventional idea of what a terraced house should look like. The 16 condominium apartments are fused like islands into an overall form with clearly defined edges. The shape clings to the contours of the existing terrain, reacting to the course of the slope with differentiated oblique angles. With its choice of materials, coloration, lack of detail, and large scale, the volume blends into the Bruggerberg Hill.

Eight simply structured 4.5- to 5.5-room apartments are arranged along the east and west sides of a central stairway. The main floor of each flat has floor-to-ceiling windows across its entire breadth, and faces onto a terrace. Rooms can optionally be separated with lightweight partition walls. The garage on the ground floor serves as a noise barrier towards the busy main street. On the other floors, stout balustrades and the closing off of the terraces at the sides create quiet and private living areas, as well as outdoor spaces.

Status
Built

Year
2013

Firm
Ken Architects

Firm location
Zurich, Switzerland

Aria Sydney, NSW, Australia

Sculptured rhythm and form is applied to an apartment complex in Bondi Junction.

Aria is located in Bondi Junction, a rapidly changing satellite CBD centered in the eastern suburbs of Sydney. Opposite a park, the project is a dynamic, sculpted apartment building that uses rhythm and form to create a positive presence on the street and in the surrounding area.

The strong visual effect was achieved by designing alternating angled balconies which sculpt the northern facade with their forms. The sculpted northern facade was further achieved through the use of detailed concrete profiles. The alternating balcony forms provide visual interest throughout the day, subtly changing with the angle and position of the sun.

The nine-story project has been designed with one apartment per floor, which provides a maximum level of privacy for the occupants. Further advantages of the single apartment strategy are solar access and natural ventilation. Winter sun penetrates deep into the north-facing living spaces. Effective cross ventilation is provided by having windows on all sides thus minimizing the need for air conditioning.

Aria is an example of how additional density can be provided in the city without compromising the benefits of a traditional-sized dwelling, even in a high density context such as Bondi Junction.

Status
Built

Year
2013

Firm
MHN Design Union

Firm location
Surry Hills, NSW, Australia

Rundeskogen Sandes, Norway

Rundeskogen apartment towers consist of 113 units of diverse typologies.

The Rundeskogen apartments are situated at an infrastructural node, linking three cities on the west coast of Norway. Single-family houses and small-scale housing projects dominate the Rogaland region, and the project shows an alternative and more compact collective living form.

The three towers contain 113 units, with the highest tower reaching 16 stories. The flats range between 645 to 1,505 square feet.

To minimize the footprint of the three towers and retain the fjord view, the first apartment floors have been lifted off the ground, cantilevering from the core and creating covered outdoor spaces.

The organizational element of the entire project is the star-shaped core structure made of concrete. The fins are extended as separation walls between the flats. On the ground, the fins and bracings of the stem-like core spread out as roots and integrate social meeting places, play and training facilities, generous entrance halls, and communal gathering spaces.

The three towers have been shaped to allow for diagonal views, and the orientation of the floor plans are also optimized according to typology and climate.

Environmental features include solar collectors on the roof, heat recovery from gray water, and ground source heat pumps.

Status
Built

Year
2013

Firm
Helen & Hard

Firm location
Oslo, Norway

Park Tower Antwerp, Belgium

Reshaping the Antwerp skyline.

The Park Tower is situated in a unique location within walking distance from the new MAS museum, the harbor district "Eilandje," the waterfront beside the river Scheldt, and the historic city center.

With a total height of 255 feet, the Park Tower is one of the highest buildings in Antwerp. The strikingly bright white exterior turns the tower into an attention-grabbing beacon that stands out as a landmark for the entire district.

The tower is a vertical reflection of a classic urban street: from the ground floor, which has a commercial function, the tower literally stacks up to host different habitation styles in the 20 higher stories. The first 10 floors are made up of 160 studios and 80 student rooms. On the next 10 floors there are 115 habitation units with elderly care facilities.

Each studio or apartment has a private terrace. To be able to use these terraces in a comfortable way, a particular wind protection concept was conceived by the architects, consisting of randomly placed glass panels. This concept allowed for the development of a playful, layered facade with a fascinating dynamic of constantly changing light and shadow. The double facade also protects privacy and reduces vertigo.

Status
Built

Year
2014

Firm
**Studio Farris
Architects**

Firm location
Antwerp, Belgium

House on a Dune Harbour Island, Bahamas

A private residence establishes a delicate, meditative space that ushers in a transition from lush tropics to wide ocean.

Harbour Island is a relaxed yet luxurious getaway perched in the surreal waters of the Atlantic edge of the Great Bahama bank. In this earnest and timeless place, the architecture for this private residence is conceived as simultaneously powerful, yet comfortable; primitive, yet innovative; casual, yet elegant; raw, yet refined. The result is a sensual experience, reduced to its essence through the use of elemental forms and sincere materiality and detailing.

The central space of the house is essentially an open breezeway, allowing visual and pedestrian connectivity across the site. Within this pavilion space there is the living and dining areas that open onto verandas protected from the elements by the deep overhangs of the gabled roof. The rest of the living spaces are simply arranged around the central space. To the left are two guest suites with private bathrooms, and to the right are the kitchen area and the master suite. Materials have been selected for their distinctive sincerity, environmental sensitivity, and a resonance with the vernacular.

This private residence establishes a delicate, meditative and mediating space that facilitates the transition from the lush tropic landscape to the wide languorous ocean.

Status
Built

Year
2013

Firm
Oppenheim Architecture+ Design

Firm location
Miami, FL, USA

House in Sai Kung Hong Kong, China

The project creates a spacious, stylish, and tranquil living space.

Peacefully nestled in the plentiful and verdant hills of Sai Kung, this 4,550-square-foot house is completely remodeled to create a spacious, stylish, and tranquil living space for its owners. The designer transformed an impractical and cramped split-level house into a four-story home, incorporating a garage, a large living room, a family room, two small en suite bedrooms, two guestrooms with one guest bathroom, a services room, a master en suite bedroom with a spacious walk-in closet and den, as well as an open rooftop sitting area with spectacular sea and garden views.

The owner wanted to provide ample space for hosting guests. Thus, the ground floor stretches from the entrance out to the backyard deck, and is separated by a large set of foldable glass patio doors overlooking a swimming pool. The design extends the open kitchen downwards, creating a clutter-free floor plan yet perfectly outfitting all the essentials. The dining table is hidden at the floor level and can be elevated when required to further enhance space usage.

A hip indoor glass garage design adds edge to the home's raw and stylish finish. The design of the house is practical, aesthetically pleasing, and fulfills its intended purpose in improving the overall lifestyle of its owners.

Status
Built

Year
2014

Firm
Millimeter Interior Design

Firm location
Hong Kong, China

The Gores Group Headquarters Beverly Hills, CA, USA

A corporate headquarters renovation re-imagined with a cross material application of pattern and form.

The Gores Group Headquarters is sited along a busy stretch of Wilshire Boulevard at the western gateway to Beverly Hills, CA. The existing condition presented a vacant 1960s office building on the lot that fronts Wilshire Blvd. to the north and an outdated, two-story parking structure across an alley to the south. The alley between the lots was expanded and a new structure was built to replace the unsound parking garage. The design utilizes the existing structure of the office building, completely upgrading all systems and interiors, and explores the idea of re-skinning an office building. This exploration resulted in the use of a cross-material patterning that unifies the project with its continuity.

The impetus of this language is the use of a mechanically ventilated, double-layer facade that consists of varied custom-slumped glass panels. The patterned interlayer sandwiched within this glass provides visual opacity gradients on the exterior and selectively filters views, privacy, and light on the interior. The patterning of this glass also translates across materials and conditions, ranging from voluptuous CNC carved stone facade elements to an airy perforated metal roof canopy. An expansive atrium was carved out of the center of the existing structure to bring ample light to the interior offices.

Status
Built

Year
2014

Firm
Belzberg Architects

Firm location
Santa Monica, CA, USA

Biodiversity Centre Granada, Spain

"The Ruin and the Tree." Architecture and landscape join together in the shade of a magnificent tree.

The building is located on the outskirts of the town of Loja (Granada, Spain), which has a unique agricultural character. The project relates to a beautiful plot of cultivated land served by an irrigation ditch and a leafy mass. The building embraces a new program based on conscientiousness, protection, and publicity of the agricultural beliefs of Loja.

The Biodiversity Centre is heavily involved in cultivation. It has an education program for farmers and high schools. In the main office area there is a zone for the treatment of seeds which are characteristic of the area. The project aims to minimize its overall presence by becoming as natural to the surroundings as possible. This effect is achieved through opening out the design and absorbing the open patio of the ancient, preexisting house.

The old ruin generates the traces of the new project, redrawing the past in the shade of the tree. The location of the building also appreciates the presence of the arboreal mass along the river. The strong conditions of the topology, including the encounter of slopes of up to 16 feet, will be solved by building a hinge between the three different platforms of the terrain.

Status
Built

Year
2012

Firm
Jose Luis Muñoz

Firm location
Granada, Spain

Zonic Vision Office Bangkok, Thailand

An office building reflects its activity through its skin.

In order to reveal the agenda of a building through its skin, Stu/D/O Architects interpreted the design for the Zonic Vision Office project through its names: 'Zonic' and 'Vision.' The architecture was delivered by conforming sound to vision using the concept of the equalizer. Stu/D/O Architects turned the equalizer's dynamic visual signal of sound frequency components into architecture by using varying intensities in the facade glazing.

In designing this visualization, the glazing of Zonic Vision was defined by three main categories: the transparent, the translucent, and the opaque. Layering the different intensities was determined by the functions of the space within. The building interior includes a commodity showroom, stock room, office space, meeting room, and a cafe. The facade composition was organized in order to reflect the different levels of privacy needed within the building. Hence, the public spaces such as the cafe and showroom use the transparent glass; the office and meeting room use the translucent skins; and the CEO office and the private garden use the opaque glazing. Two compact spaces were concaved out from the form to host small trees in order to create a better working environment.

Status
Built

Year
2014

Firm
Stu/D/O Architects

Firm location
Bangkok, Thailand

China Merchants Tower & Woods Park Master Plan Shenzhen, China

The China Merchants Tower: a beacon for Shenzhen.

The China Merchants Tower anchors the Woods Park master plan, located in the Nanshan District of Shenzhen, China. The tower's tapered form increases the building's aspect ratio and allows lower floors to slope away from the sun, decreasing the solar radiation on the exterior wall.

The tower features a low-E, unitized glass curtain wall that is clad in a system of horizontal glass fins. The facade's fins have been closely spaced together in order to reduce solar gain. Aesthetically, the fins give the facade a fine-grain texture and balance the slenderness generated by the tower's verticality. They also bounce daylight deep into the space and refract light at night, working in conjunction with the top of the tower to illuminate the form.

The China Merchants Tower incorporates a comprehensive suite of environmental features that contribute to its performance and target a two-star certification from the China Green Star rating system. The suite includes efficient water fixtures and gray water management that produce water savings of up to 25 percent; a central plan with variable speed chillers, pumps, drive fans, and zoning controls; and an efficient curtain wall that works in tandem with the shading fin system to reduce solar heat gain.

Status
Built

Year
2013

Firm
Skidmore, Owings & Merrill

Firm location
Chicago, IL, USA

One World Trade Center New York, NY, USA

One World Trade Center: Reclaiming the New York skyline and establishing a new civic icon for the city and country.

One World Trade Center recaptures the New York skyline, reasserts downtown Manhattan's preeminence as a business center, and establishes a new civic icon for the country. It is a memorable architectural landmark for the city and the nation, combining simplicity and clarity of form. Extending the long tradition of American ingenuity in high-rise construction, the design solution is an innovative mix of architecture, structure, urban design, safety, and sustainability.

One World Trade Center is a bold icon in the sky that acknowledges the adjacent memorial. While the memorial, carved out of the earth, speaks of the past and of remembrance, One World Trade Center speaks to the future as it rises upward in a faceted form filled with, and reflecting, light.

As the tower rises from a cubic base, its edges are chamfered back, resulting in a faceted form composed of eight elongated isosceles triangles. At its middle, the tower forms a perfect octagon in plan and then culminates in a glass parapet whose plan is a 150-foot-by-150-foot square, rotated 45 degrees from the base. As the sun moves through the sky, the surfaces appear like a kaleidoscope, and will change throughout the day as light and weather conditions change.

Status
Built

Year
2014

Firm
Skidmore, Owings & Merrill

Firm location
New York, NY, USA

Office > Entropy, Echoing Green Corporate Headquarters
New York, NY, USA

An office designed to move from one space in NY to the next, using the same architecture but deployed in a different way

This project is an office space design that was meant to operate in two states of being. In its first state, Taylor and Miller designed and fabricated a very basic set of six architectural units (different sizes of plywood boxes and associated desk surfaces) that would stack and interlock. The deployment of the boxes was intentionally more disordered; exposing holes and creating areas of porosity from one area to the next.

In the office's second state, the exact same basic set of architectural units were deployed, but in a different manner. In the second state, the units were distributed throughout the space very categorically; for example, all small boxes were stacked together, all long boxes were stacked together. In essence, the design elements were composed in this space to be more ordered.

For the designers, the idea was that as the office expanded and added more workforce to the new space, there would be a certain level of disorder associated with the increased density of people and overlapping tasks. The architectural system was designed to offset this move towards disorder, with the repetitive texture screens dividing one workspace from the next to provide a quiet layering of space and privacy.

Status
Built

Year
2014

Firm
Taylor and Miller

Firm location
Brooklyn, NY, USA

Architect's Office at Kim Yam Road Singapore

The design direction for this new workplace is largely driven by a reaction against the rigidity of the typical bureau.

The clients had just moved out of a typical office building in the Central Business District and were searching for a new space that would not just accommodate their expansion, but also reflect the philosophy of their creative pursuits.

The site is an old barrel-vaulted library hall of a former school building built in the 1960s. The clients recognized the immense potential of the site in the early stages of the hall's redevelopment. The resulting design sensitively implements modern functionality within the existing building. The design direction is largely driven by the responses to the site and the client's requirements to enhance and activate the genius loci of the site, and to achieve an expression of an "Anti-Office." By combining these approaches, the designers sought to create an alternative and creative environment imbued by the spirit of the place.

Seeking to celebrate and activate the intrinsic qualities of the existing space, the scheme is conceived as an orchestration of varied and contextually sensitive spatial experiences, instead of the function-centric approach typical of office design.

The design rejects the rigidity of the typical bureau in favor of a creative environment that challenges conventions, celebrates informal spaces, and revels in the masquerade of commonplace office functions.

Status
Built

Year
2013

Firm
Park + Associates

Firm location
Singapore

Wild Turkey Bourbon Visitor Center Lawrenceburg, KY, USA

A distillery's visitor center focuses on product rebranding and an immersive visitor experience inspired by its context.

Located on a bluff overlooking the Kentucky River, the Visitor Center is the newest component of recent additions and expansions to the Wild Turkey Distillery Complex, one of seven original member distilleries of the Kentucky Bourbon Trail. The 9,140-square-foot facility houses interactive exhibits, a gift shop, event venues, a tasting room, and ancillary support spaces. In concert with a major rebranding program under new ownership (Gruppo Campari), the project specifically focuses on exploring possibilities for reinforcing the new direction in product rebranding and marketing efforts. The project also aims to provide an immersive, interactive visitor experience that capitalizes on the dramatic landscape. Referencing the specificity of place and context through regional building traditions is also important to the design.

Utilizing a simple barn silhouette, the building presents a recognizable marker at the scale of the landscape. Clad in a custom chevron pattern of stained wood siding, the simplicity of the barn form is contrasted by the intricacy of the building skin at closer range. Alternating areas of light-filtering lattice blur the boundaries between inside/out and light/dark. By night, the solidity of the dark structure transforms into a delicate, glowing lantern of filigree perched above the river.

Status
Built

Year
2013

Firm
De Leon & Primmer Architecture Workshop

Firm location
Louisville, KY, USA

Wollongong Central Expansion Wollongong, NSW, Australia

A retail design opportunity as a catalyst for urban transformation.

The five-story, 600,000-square-foot Wollongong Central shopping center creates a renewed social heart and retail destination that fuses architecture, art, and culture.

The project's built form connects the northern and southern parts of the city via a five-level 'Public Street,' knitting together existing and future parts of the city, enlivening once quiet streets, and promoting new growth.

The Illawarra (the region Wollongong is located in) is characterized by a unique dichotomy: a perception of being a tough and gritty town defined solely by its history as a steel town, and its beautiful landscape between the rainforest escarpment and the Pacific Ocean. This friction defines the architecture of the building. A precise outer shell reflects the man-made elements that unfold to a warm, organic interior-scape that celebrates the natural.

The facade evokes the drama of the cliffs that dominate the coastline, featuring jagged steel blades and fractured glass reinforced concrete forms. An abstraction of the Illawarra flame tree is embedded into the concrete, and at night, the facade transforms into an illuminated constellation of flowers.

This connection of the built form out (rather than the typical inward looking model) was vitally important in establishing a cohesive response to the life of the street and of the city.

Status
Built

Year
2014

Firm
HDR|Rice Daubney

Firm location
Sydney, NSW, Australia

Ring of Celestial Bliss Hsinchu, Taiwan

The main lantern of the Taiwan Lantern Festival is inspired by local characteristics.

The main lantern of the Taiwan Lantern Festival is aptly themed 'Ring of Celestial Bliss.'

From the outside, the lantern appears as a glowing object hovering in the night, a feat achieved through the special and innovative design of the steel structure. Inside the lantern, a ring of constantly moving images produced by the latest projection technology and LED lighting, which serve as a metaphor for nature's endless cycle of life, inspire hope for the future. Furthermore, the shifting inclination of the screens leads to a more dynamic viewing experience.

The choice of form and materials used for the lantern is inspired by the historical and cultural characteristics of Hsinchu, whose ancient name is the City of Bamboo Walls. While reusable steel is the primary structural component, the outer cladding consists of bamboo trunks. The inner projection screen is made of recycled materials, and bamboo tubes are used as a permeable flooring material. The bamboo will be collected after the end of the lantern festival and donated to 'Earth Passengers' workshop to build the environmental education classrooms in Taitung.

'Ring of Celestial Bliss,' inspired by local characteristics and executed with Taiwanese technology and design, conveys a profound respect for nature while providing an auspicious vision for the future.

Status
Built

Year
2013

Firm
J.J.Pan & Partners

Firm location
Taipei, Taiwan

Design Republic Design Commune Shanghai, China

A design by Neri&Hu Design and Research Office in the center of Shanghai, China.

Design Republic Design Commune, located in the center of Shanghai, envisions itself as a gathering space for designers and design patrons to admire, ponder, exchange, and learn. It houses the new flagship store for Design Republic, a modern furniture retailer, alongside a mixture of design-focused retail concepts, including books, fashion, lighting, accessories, and flowers. The Commune will also have a design gallery, an event space, a cafe, a restaurant by Michelin-Starred Chef Jason Atherton, and a one-bedroom Design Republic apartment.

Situated within the historic relic of the Police Headquarters built by the British in the 1910s, the project takes a surgical approach to renovation.

Neri&Hu replaced the rather dilapidated row shops on the street front with a modern, glassy insertion onto the brick facade. The street level periphery is enveloped by transparent glazing to reveal the existing brick work and rough concrete structures. Breathing new life into a traditional colonial building plan, Neri&Hu strategically removed certain floor plates, walls, and ceiling panels to allow a renewed experience of the existing building.

Various small and precise incisions have been made in the interior architecture to reveal the building's history and integrity while creating intersections for a coherent experience when moving through the building.

Status
Built

Year
2012

Firm
Neri&Hu Design and Research Office

Firm location
Shanghai, China

63

Óbidos Technological Park Central Building Óbidos, Portgal

The project defines an inhabited topography on which a square-shaped ring rests.

On the axis between Lisbon and Coimbra, the Óbidos Technological Park aims to link academic research with business production. The design for the main building defines an inhabited topography on which a square-shaped ring rests. All the public spaces, such as the main meeting and multipurpose room, shops, restaurant, and a "fablab" are purposely located on the ground floor in order to reinforce the public character of the interior void. Working areas are distributed on the first floor on a modular grid that allows greater flexibility in the use of the space.

   Three main materials are used: concrete, steel, and glass. The ground floor is all about rough concrete, expressing a telluric structure. In contrast to the ground floor, the first floor is all about geometry and precision. A set of huge metal trusses, assembled to create four voided and interconnected prisms, build a large and floating cloister. The building spans a total of 44,090 square feet.

   The decision to imbed part of the program underneath the landscape achieves several sustainability goals. The first goal is to increase the green surfaces within the plot, and the second goal is to decrease energy needs in terms of AVAC systems for cooling or warming the building.

Status
Built

Year
2014

Firm
**Jorge Mealha
Arquitecto**

Firm location
Cascais, Portugal

Óbidos Technological Park Central Building Óbidos, Portgal

Bombay Sapphire Distillery Laverstoke Mill, Hampshire, UK

Heatherwick Studio transformed an old paper mill at Laverstoke into Bombay Sapphire's first in-house production facility.

The gin-maker Bombay Sapphire commissioned the creation of the company's first in-house production facility. Formerly a water-powered paper mill, the site contained more than 40 derelict buildings, which have been regenerated and restored as part of Heatherwick Studio's master plan. Central to the development of the master plan is the River Test. Contained within a narrow high-sided concrete channel and largely covered over, the river had become almost invisible as the site developed over many years.

The river was widened, its banks opened out and planted in order to transform it into a route that draws visitors through the site to a newly defined courtyard at its center.

Heatherwick Studio's master plan proposed the creation of two new greenhouses to grow the 10 exotic plant species used in the distillation process. These greenhouses, one tropical and one Mediterranean climate, emerge from the northern still house to sit within the waters of the widened river. The connection to the still house allows waste heat from the distillation process to be recycled to maintain the warm climates for the plant species to flourish.

This new botanical distillery has achieved a BREEAM 'outstanding' rating for sustainability, the first facility in the drinks manufacturing industry to be awarded this rating.

Status
Built

Year
2014

Firm
Heatherwick Studio

Firm location
London, UK

Knot House Geoje, South Korea

Five sculptural vacation houses rest on a cliff on the southern coast of Geoje Island, South Korea.

Five white, sculptural buildings rest on a cliff on the southern coast of Geoje Island, South Korea. The white walls of the buildings fold into themselves to create a private ocean view from each house. Tall pine trees that grow between the buildings and the sea occasionally frame the views.

The two-story Knot House at the top is a clubhouse as well as the owner's residence. At the border of the clubhouse, a V-shaped infinity pool merges with the ocean. Four additional one-story Knot Houses host six guest rooms. The narrow, long strip of the building site provided an initial challenge to fit the maximum number of units while maintaining privacy and ocean views. Atelier Chang suggested a layout which turned each house by 40 degrees toward the sea. This staggering allows an unrestricted ocean view for the guests and produces niches of private zones.

The knotted folding and unfolding creates different apertures in and outside the building. Where the knot unfolds in the front, 10- to 16-foot full height windows open toward the ocean view. Additionally, where the knot gets most loose, an intimate experience of bathing flows out to the exterior garden, blurring the boundary between inside and outside.

Status
Built

Year
2014

Firm
Atelier Chang

Firm location
London, UK

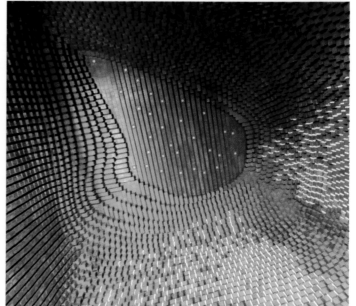

Brick Spris Coffe Tehran, Iran

A new 300-square-foot cafe located in Tehran.

Spris Cafe is located in Tehran with a total area of 300 square feet. The cafe is surrounded by Iranian handicrafts shops, and neighbors the Iranian Handicrafts Organization.

    The design incorporates elements of traditional Iranian architectural design, as well as a materiality concept based on an integrated geometry that flows continuously from outside to inside. The design also introduces unique brick and light patterning via a 3D design.

    The turquoise, blue-glazed bricks face south, and are shaped with the integrated geometry of tailored bricklaying that was created by the 3D design. The choice of material is inspired from Iranian traditional architecture to introduce an identity for the project, and avoid using a variety of materials to emphasize the integration of the form.

    The exterior lighting consists of lamps illuminating the gaps in between the joints of the bricks, which is inspired by Iranian traditional architecture but also translates into a modern effect.

    The final goal was to develop a simple technique for construction in order for builders to be able to achieve results in a short period of time by following the tailored, step-by-step method introduced for the project.

Status
Built

Year
2014

Firm
Hooba Design

Firm location
Tehran, Iran

Restaurant Steirereck Vienna, Austria

A place of indulgence and recreation in Vienna's city center.

The Steirereck is one of the best restaurants in the world. Despite renovations being completed only a few years before, a comprehensive reformulation of the restaurant became necessary. The winning competition design takes the individual tables as a starting point. The special table arrangement, the large electric sash windows, and the slightly reflective metal facade, which appears to be coated with dew, all evoke a sense of being outside and yet also at home.

Guests also experience the highest levels of acoustic and thermal comfort. The material of the pavilion's facade is brought into the interior of the existing dining space, enabling rooms of differing sizes and proportions to be created according to need by means of rotatable elements. The ceiling floats above the dining space like a horizontal contour map, shaped by the possible positions of the rotatable panels. The middle section, where the guests and personnel meet, is decorated with a tile pattern reminiscent of a kitchen, which, together with the cabinets filled with kitchen items, gives guests the sense that they are involved in the culinary center.

The result is something new but also cozy, something that merges into the background but yet is a strong architectural statement.

Status
Built

Year
2014

Firm
PPAG architects

Firm location
Vienna, Austria

Abenoma Bar Osaka, Japan

Swaths of crumpled tracing paper cocoon the interior of this pop-up bar in a Japanese gallery in order to transform the space.

This is a project in which young designers met and collaborated in order to make a place where people get together in Abeno, Osaka. There used to be a row house in a back alley in Abeno and now it has been converted and remodeled into a gallery space called 'Abenoma.' We produced a self-built space by using the uncommon but simple material of tracing paper with local residents. This huge space made of paper is akin to a secret base and turns into a bar at night.

The project was achieved by folding, pasting, crumpling, and sticking paper together to make a space with the goal of bringing people together as well.

Status
Built

Year
2014

Firm
Naoya Matsumoto Design

Firm location
Osaka, Japan

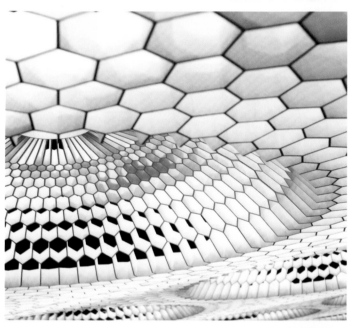

PM Club Sofia, Bulgaria

If God is a DJ, PM club is a music temple.

PM is a night club for music lovers situated on an area of 5,380 square feet. At the entrance one is greeted by a composition of domes. The dome has structural independence and also provides additional space for the interior. In our project, domes are also used to conceal the concrete beams on the ceiling and to create 'invisible' ventilation. We made the domes transparent, which allows them to display 1,500 pixels of a state-of-the-art light mural.

In every temple there is an altar. In this case the altar is the DJ booth. We intentionally strengthened the architectural perspective to put an accent on the DJ. The main bar is situated in the middle which helped to further develop zones in the club and create the "forced movement" around it. Near the entrance we looked for constriction of space that is immediately released towards the scene evoking the laws of fluid dynamics in physics. This solution directs people inside towards the scene and eliminates crowding in the most neuralgic point: the entrance.

The whole interior was designed in black and bathed in light. All the equipment and furniture are custom-designed to create the unique identity of the club.

Status
Built

Year
2014

Firm
Studio Mode

Firm location
Sofia, Bulgaria

Maggie's Merseyside at Clatterbridge Merseyside, UK

A temporary Maggie's Cancer Care Centre.

The project is a cancer care center at Clatterbridge Hospital in Merseyside, commissioned and operated by Maggie's Cancer Care Trust. Although one of many Maggie's centers across the UK, this building is special as it is the first ever temporary center. The building has created a place of support for patients and their families until a permanent Maggie's Centre is delivered in central Liverpool.

In order to achieve the tight budget, six redundant site cabins were dramatically transformed into one single building. A pavilion that was used during the London 2012 Olympics was also repurposed, with its 32-foot-long window revealing wonderful views over the local landscape. These structures were arranged around several existing trees on the site, creating a series of courtyards.

The Maggie's Centre is given privacy from the rest of the hospital by a scalloped fiber-glass screen which wraps the entire perimeter of the building. Large windows focus views over fields or to secluded gardens, and the walls are lined in curved timber moldings to provide a warm and welcoming interior.

The great success of this project has been to realize a building within strict constraints and with limited means, and which now provides invaluable care and support for people dealing with cancer.

Status
Built

Year
2014

Firm
Carmody Groarke

Firm location
London, UK

Grotto Georgian Bay, Ontario, Canada

Vision, technology, and old-world craft combine to form a transcendent sauna integrated with the Canadian landscape.

The deep blue waters of Lake Huron and glacially sculpted rock formations seduce visitors to this remote wilderness. Located several hours north of Toronto, Canada, the area is characterized by numerous islands and protected natural land. Perched at the northwest edge of the site, the Grotto Sauna pushes architecture to the limits of imagination. Grottos form secret internal worlds within the simplest looking rock formations, their interiors carved by natural forces to create sublime worlds of complexity, wonder, and delight.

The project had a great number of technical and logistical challenges. Saunas as a building type are particularly challenging, requiring a high degree of precision to perform optimally, while withstanding extreme heat and humidity. In this instance, these extreme parameters were compounded by the location at the edge of the lake, facing ice flows in the winter and rising water levels in the summer. We wrote the scripting language for the wood forms and worked directly with the fabricators to develop a methodology for making the panels. In addition, the site is located on a rocky island peninsula, a three-hour barge trip from the nearest town. Thus, the decision was made to prefabricate the sauna in Toronto and deliver it by barge and crane to the site.

Status
Built

Year
2014

Firm
Partisan Projects

Firm location
Toronto, Ontario, Canada

Lidingövallen Lidingö, Stockholm, Sweden

A small soccer stadium for Lidingö Football Club.

When the municipality moved their secretariat out of their current location, the IFK Lidingö Football Club needed a new office, as well as locker rooms and a café to serve as a meeting place.

Sited between existing lighting masts and a grove of pine trees, a narrow strip along the main soccer field was just enough space to house a new structure. Since the field lacked stands for spectators, the project not only fulfilled the brief but also added seating on the roof of the building.

Inspired by the classic leather soccerball, the hexagon was the guiding principle for the design. The building is split in two, divided by a passage from the parking area and space for outdoor seating for the café, which is in the northern part along with offices and assembly spaces. The southern part of the building houses locker rooms and a laundry room.

Due to the low budget, the materials had to be simple yet robust: plywood, concrete, stoneware tiles, and wood wool panels for the interior; checker plate, treated wood, and fiber cement for the exterior.

Commissioned by a small club with limited resources, the project turned out to be a big success and is appreciated by the whole community.

Status
Built

Year
2014

Firm
DinellJohansson

Firm location
Stockholm, Sweden

Jeonbuk Hyundai Motors FC Clubhouse Jeollabuk-do, South Korea

Jeonbuk Hyundai FC Clubhouse is a dynamic, efficient sports facility that basks in the beauty of its site.

Just as a game of soccer requires strategic passes, powerful striking, and eleven members that move and breathe as one body, successful architecture also requires a coalescence of key ingredients. In designing the Jeonbuk Hyundai Motors FC Clubhouse, Suh Architects incorporated efficient circulation, distinctive communal spaces, outdoor courtyards, and customized architectural details. These elements were arranged strategically to allow for natural sunlight, fresh air, and panoramic views to penetrate all areas. Despite the building's linear expression, the layout features a 'one-stop' system yielding minimized distances and easily accessible facilities.

The building plan is programmatically driven by the training, rehabilitation, and recreational needs of its resident players and staff. The complex features two outdoor soccer fields, one indoor soccer field, a fitness center, state-of-the-art-aquatic rehabilitation rooms, main and reserved players' locker rooms, recreational areas, resident rooms, and public and private outdoor courtyard-garden areas. The building's overall mass and orientation seeks to embrace the site's expansive views of rolling mountains without dominating its surroundings. Its leaning, stone and metal-clad exterior symbolize the speed and force of the game of soccer as well as the vision of a company willing to build a winning team alongside its own future identity.

Status
Built

Year
2013

Firm
Suh Architects

Firm location
Seoul, South Korea

WMS Boathouse at Clark Park Chicago, IL, USA

By offering new public access to the Chicago River, the boathouse catalyzes its recreational and ecological revival.

Located in a public park, the boathouse serves people from all over the city, especially young people. It also serves as a home base for rowing clubs.

The program of field house and boat storage was divided into two distinct structures. This design strategy helped the project stay within its modest budget by detaching the fully conditioned assembly space of the two-story field house from the simpler function of the single-story boat storage building. With its indoor rowing tank and ergometer room, the field house accommodates year-round training programs, providing space for team practice, youth fitness, and courses for people with disabilities. The single-story boat storage building houses rental kayaks and canoes as well as the teams' rowing shells.

The overall goal of health led the design team to focus on efficient energy use and the water quality of the river. The boathouse's clerestory roof lets daylight warm the floor slab in winter and provides for ventilation in summer. In combination with geothermal wells, this method of passive solar heating and natural ventilation uses 57 percent less energy than the median EUI for public assembly recreation buildings. The roof's form and the design of the site together function as the storm-water management system, diverting 100 percent of runoff from the sewer.

Status
Built

Year
2013

Firm
Studio Gang Architects

Firm location
Chicago, IL, USA

Ski Jumps Planica, Slovenia

The Planica sport facility is designed to exist in harmony with the natural environment.

The main focus of the design is based on the profound relationship between construction, constructed site, and natural site. The Planica sport facility lies at the forefoot of Slovenia's largest natural protected area, and is one of most exciting entry points into the Triglav National Park. The precise planning, the systematic selection and reduction of materials, and bold shapes and forms all align with the exciting silhouette of the mountains and the pine and beech forest. The project hinges on multiple relationships: solid versus soft, resistant versus ephemeral, cold versus warm, and monumental versus intimate. The changes in the natural seasons are also an influence, as cold, sharp mountains refer to the simple geometry of the concrete structures, and the colors of late summer are revealed in the exposed wooden details.

Ski jump facilities are normally designed to facilitate large competitions with enormous infrastructure and logistics. When more than 15,000 people come to this fragile valley, the form of the architecture ceases to be the focus as its operational function holds the central role. However, for the everyday situation, when only a few of the young ski jumpers come to train in solitude, the simplicity, respect toward the site, and robustness of the project is awakened.

Status
Built

Year
2013

Firm
Abiro

Firm location
Ljubljana, Slovenia

Moesgaard Museum Højbjerg, Denmark

The new architecture of the Moesgaard Museum supports the vision that this is more than a museum.

The new Moesgaard Museum grows out of the hilly landscape of Skåde outside Aarhus, Denmark. The new museum offers scenic views, public spaces, and first-class exhibitions on cultural history.

   With its bright courtyard gardens, terraces, and small cave-like houses, the museum invites various new and alternative types of exhibition. The heart of the building is the foyer with a cafe and outdoor service. From the foyer, the terraced underworld opens up to the light that streams in from the roof garden and the impressive view of Aarhus Bay.

   The museum acts as a public space too; in the summer, the angular projection will host a range of outdoor activities, such as lectures and traditional Midsummer Day bonfires.

   The interior of the new Moesgaard Museum is designed as a varied terrace landscape. Moesgaard Museum is a multifunctional house of culture and knowledge. The museum collaborates with the University of Aarhus and employs more than 150 museum staff and university faculty members.

   The overall sustainable strategy has been integrated in the architectural design. The compact building volume is integrated into the landscape. The rectangular, sloping roof, oriented towards the south, reduces the facade area and brings daylight through the rising northern end and sides facing east and west.

Status
Built

Year
2014

Firm
Henning Larsen Architects

Firm location
Copenhagen, Denmark

The Blue Planet Kastrup, Denmark

Inspired by water in endless motion, The Blue Planet aquarium's architecture tells the story of what awaits inside.

Inspired by water in endless motion, the new Danish national aquarium, The Blue Planet, is shaped like a giant whirlpool.

The Blue Planet is located on an elevated headland towards the sea, north of Kastrup Harbor. Located by the seaside, the whirlpool shape connects sea and landscape. The facade is covered with small diamond-shaped aluminum plates, which adapt to the building's organic form. Just like water, aluminum reflects the colors and light of the sky and thus the building's expression varies with the changes in its natural surroundings.

Visitors reach the entrance by following the first and longest of the whirlpool's whirls. With a smooth transition, the landscape passes into the building, while the outdoor ponds denote the unique experience that awaits the aquarium visitors as they enter The Blue Planet.

The circular foyer is the central point of navigation in the aquarium. Here visitors choose which river, lake, or ocean to explore. By enabling multiple routes, the risk of queues in front of individual aquariums is reduced. Each exhibition has its own theme and entrance from the foyer, where sound and images are used to introduce the atmosphere of the different exhibitions.

Status
Built

Year
2013

Firm
3XN

Firm location
Copenhagen, Denmark

Telfair Studio Lyme, CT, USA

A painting studio sited in the rural flood plain of the Connecticut River.

Built on a rural site overlooking the Connecticut River, this studio was commissioned by an artist who paints large-scale, imagined landscape paintings. We wondered whether the building could evoke the landscape, and express the resonance between the work being produced inside the studio and the surrounding context.

We created a deep-set shadowed eave, invoking the horizon, which is omnipresent in the artist's work. Above the eave is a matte, anodized aluminum roof that evenly reflects the sky. Below the eave are blackened cedar walls, mimicking the dark wooded trees that backdrop the building. The site is a flood zone, therefore the studio floor sits above grade and extends to a wooden deck surrounding the structure, floating just above the tall native grasses.

The artist works on several paintings at a time, incorporating similar tones into each series. The main studio space is therefore scaled in plan and volume to accommodate her method of working. She requires mostly opaque walls, however the studio offers calculated views to the outside without allowing direct sunlight to enter the space. These vertical openings frame a single view through the entire building toward a lone grove of river birch trees. Two large banks of skylights frame the sky.

Status
Built

Year
2013

Firm
Peterson Rich Office

Firm location
Brooklyn, NY, USA

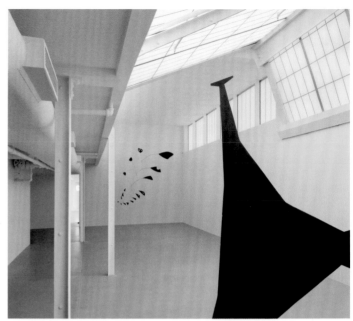

Calder Foundation Project Space New York, NY, USA

A flexible art space designed for exhibitions, installations, performances, and lectures.

The Calder Foundation Project Space is a 7,500-square-foot flexible art space designed for exhibitions, installations, performances, and lectures. The structure, transformed by STEPHANIEGOTO and located atop a 12-story commercial building in New York's Chelsea neighborhood, was formerly three contiguous structures that made up a 1920s print-block making studio.

Goto unified the one-story structures with a custom-fabricated facade composed of triangular metal panels made from a blue interference coated and bead blasted stainless steel. She stripped the building to its original bones, opening and redefining the interior spaces into distinct experiences. Natural light used in harmony with white walls and a matte concrete floor allow the interior space to glow with ambient light.

The three existing mansard-type skylight roofs were transformed and redefined. The first roof was conceived as a skylight, bringing light from above; the second as a solid flat roof with clerestories, bringing side light; and the third as a solid roof with five 12-foot-tall windows, inviting the northern light.

Additional design moments include bathroom walls detailed in triangular black granite tiles that reference the exterior facade, an exterior roof surface defined by recycled rubber tiles with the same triangular geometry, and two steel porthole doors cut into thick exterior walls to the outdoor art space.

Status
Built

Year
2012

Firm
STEPHANIEGOTO

Firm location
New York, NY, USA

Carnal Hall at Le Rosey Rolle, Switzerland

Under a sustainable, reflective metal dome, a state of the art concert hall made of recycled wood.

Under a reflective, low metal dome, this 900-seat concert hall is entirely made of recycled OSB compressed wood, together with natural mechanical ventilation (and no AC!). Located by Lake Geneva in the provincial town of Rolle, the renowned Swiss international boarding school known as Le Rosey is one of Europe's most esteemed educational institutions.

Despite a tight budget, the objectives for the concert hall were ambitious: to provide a world-class auditorium that is equally capable of responding to the most stringent sustainability requirements and welcoming the most prestigious orchestras in the world. The program for a new performing arts facility included a 900-seat concert hall, black-box theater, conference rooms, rehearsal and practice spaces, a library and learning center, a restaurant, cafe, student lounge, and various other amenities.

The proportions and shallow rake of the concert hall create reflections from the sides and back of the hall generating an intimate sound in all seats. The hall is also adaptable for film projection, lectures, and amplified music.

Similarly, exceptional measures were taken to ensure the building met sustainability goals. Passive air ventilation systems were utilized throughout the building: natural air is channeled from the outside to ventilate the concert hall, and vertical facades ensure that each room has operable windows.

Status
Built

Year
2014

Firm
Bernard Tschumi Architects

Firm location
New York, NY, USA

Wallis Annenberg Center for the Performing Arts Beverly Hills, CA, USA

Rather than imitate the existing architecture, the new interventions on the site of the Wallis Annenberg Center celebrate the history of a Historic Post Office Site.

The program for the Wallis Annenberg Center for the Performing Arts (the Wallis) was to transform the Historic Post Office Site into a cultural center for the performing arts, including the 500-seat Goldsmith Theatre, the 120 seat Lovelace Studio Theatre, an education wing, administrative offices, a café, a gift shop, a sculpture garden, an education court, and state-of-the-art performing arts support spaces.

Conventional wisdom had the main programmatic element, the 500-seat theater, inserted into the original mail workroom of the historic post office, while adding a wing to house all the other pertinent programmatic elements. However, we thought of a new way. It was our contention to reutilize the historic post office without major alterations by inserting the ancillary programmatic elements within it and building an annex to house the new Goldsmith Theatre. This program resulted in a better use of space. Furthermore, it required fewer modifications to the historic aspects of the original post office. This concept enabled us to fully restore the major elements of the post office's historic fabric utilizing the Secretary of Interior Standards while maintaining eligibility and historic tax credit status.

Status
Built

Year
2013

Firm
SPF:architects

Firm location
Culver City, CA, USA

Hy-Fi Queens, NY, USA

A paradigm for design and construction with almost no waste, energy, or carbon emissions.

Hy-Fi, commissioned by the Museum of Modern Art and MoMA PS1, is a circular tower of organic bricks. The structure is an extension of the natural Carbon Cycle, with a revolutionary new construction material that grows out of living materials and returns to the earth through composting at the end of the structure's lifecycle. In contrast to short-sighted architecture, it is designed to disappear as much as it is designed to appear.

Our project uses biological technologies combined with advanced computation and engineering to create a new construction material, a new method of bio-design, and a building that is almost 100 percent grown and 100 percent compostable.

We designed a new type of brick through an innovative combination of corn stalk waste and living mushrooms. This organic mixture grows into solid bricks in five days with no added energy. The bricks are low cost and extremely sustainable. When our building is deconstructed, the bricks are composted and the resulting soil is used by local community gardens.

Our building offers a familiar yet new structure in the context of the glass towers and typical brick construction of New York City. Overall, the structure offers shade, light, views, and a future-oriented experience that is refreshing, thought-provoking, and full of wonder and optimism.

Status
Built

Year
2014

Firm
The Living

Firm location
Brooklyn, NY, USA

Vermilion Sands West Vancouver, BC, Canada

An unprecedented use of hydro-seeding to create a living pavilion for an arts festival that is ethereal and atmospheric.

Vermilion Sands is a temporary pavilion for a summer arts festival. The project uses hydro-seeding, a common method for planting large areas like freeway embankments, to create a living canopy that blurs the distinction between nature and artifice. In order to provide a shaded space during the day and an ethereal social space at night, the canopy is comprised of 260 custom-fabricated modules. Each module is shaped from a geotextile fabric, which was hydro-seeded with either clover or ryegrass, and then suspended from a grid of aircraft cable.

To irrigate the plants, an array of 150 nozzles are integrated into the canopy. The mist sustains the plants while offering adiabatic cooling for users. At the same time, LED lighting is incorporated into the columns to uplight the modules and misting plumes.

"Vermilion Sands" is the title of a collection of sci-fi short stories by J.G. Ballard. Each story focuses on a particular design or artistic medium in which nature is hybridized with technology to produce magical results. Within our Anthropocene, in which the ability to disentangle the natural from the artificial is fleeting, we can only hope that the sustainability of the future will be increasingly populated with designs akin to those in Ballard's prescient texts.

Status
Built

Year
2014

Firm
Matthew Soules Architecture

Firm location
West Vancouver, BC, Canada

Chapel in Joá Rio de Janeiro, Brazil

Built on a very sloped site, what initially seemed to be a handicap for this project showed the way for a simple structural solution.

The chapel sits on the existing access pathway and is supported by a single column opposite the entrance, which rises from the ground and transforms itself into a cross at floor level. The main steel structure supports a sequence of parallel timber porticoes that progressively change the interior spatial proportion from horizontal to vertical. The focal point is the steel cross, framed by wood and with the sea as a backdrop.

A skin of transparent glass protects the sides of the chapel and reflects the surrounding tropical forest. Seemingly floating on air, the building and its furnishings achieve a search for simplicity.

Status
Built

Year
2014

Firm
Bernardes Arquitetura

Firm location
São Paulo, Brazil

Community Church Knarvik Knarvik, Norway

The characteristic, angular shape of the new Community Church in Knarvik has become a landmark of its region.

The new Community Church in Knarvik, located on the scenic west coast of Norway, is built on a site overlooking the cultural landscape and local town center. The building is carefully adapted to an existing hillside, providing the church with an inspiring context of the surrounding heath landscape.

Inspired by the local tradition of Norwegian stave churches, the building utilizes clear and elemental geometries, materials, and constructions. The compact building volume is split into two stories on a rectangular plan, separating the sacred spaces above from the cultural and administrative functions below. An internal church square connects the two levels with an atrium stair into a continuous space, and may be joined or separated from the sanctuary with sliding glass walls to accommodate more than 500 people.

Wood is the key material of the project, expressed in the homogeneous cladding of pre-weathered pine heartwood and mirrored by the light-colored pine finish on all interior surfaces. The building has lancet-reminiscent tall and narrow windows, splayed in plan to maximize admittance of sunlight and reduce glare.

The church aspires to provide a platform for a safe upbringing for children and youth, to become a local venue for gatherings and faith, and to facilitate art, music, and cultural development.

Status
Built

Year
2014

Firm
Reiulf Ramstad Architects

Firm location
Oslo, Norway

School Floating in the Sky Sangkhlaburi, Kanchanaburi, Thailand

Located near the border of Myanmar, a school aims to alleviate poverty in the Thai village of Sangkhlaburi.

This school aims to help alleviate poverty in Sangkhlaburi village, Thailand. Located near the border of Myanmar, there are many immigrants and orphans in the area.

Wanting to provide a good future for these kids, the children were asked by their teacher to envision the school of their dreams. One of them drew a flying ship, which was then translated into the design. The image was adapted into two main architectural components: the round 'earth bag' volumes on the ground floor and a light steel structure finished with bamboo and a grass roof.

The earth bag domes are thought of as a launching pad that supplies the ship with the energy of mother earth. The upper steel building is the ship that is soaring in the sky.

The round volumes create a warm interior, fostering a sense of comfort for the children in the prayer dome and classroom. The floating level above functions as a Buddhist room and learning area. Since its completion, the school has become a successful place for the community to enjoy studying, playing, and praying everyday. The interpretation of the children's dreams into an architectural form establishes a foundation to help lead the children to a bright future.

Status
Built

Year
2013

Firm
D Environmental Design System Laboratory

Firm location
Kami, Kochi, Japan

Kaleidoscope Kindergarten Porto Cristo, Mallorca, Spain

A Kaleidoscope Kindergarten.

A transformation of a squash court in a kindergarten in Mallorca uses the traditional toy concept of the kaleidoscope. Variables such as natural light and children on the move generate a set of light reflections, constantly modifying the space and creating multiple worlds for interaction.

The kaleidoscopic structure has a hexagonal section that is 30 feet in length and six feet high, allowing children to walk inside and interact with the entirety of the space. The structure is characterized by a kaleidoscopic pink hue, a color of relaxed excitement, further contributing to the creation of this dream-like space. A random pattern of white circles of different sizes house various applications such as lighting, storage, slates, caches, and entries to other spaces.

Additional spaces such as a bath, staircase, the Magic Room, the Periscope, and the mezzanine respond to various sensory experiences playing with spaces, colors, reflections, textures, and fluorescence.

Status
Built

Year
2014

Firm
A2arquitectos

Firm location
Madrid, Spain

TianTai No.2 Primary School Tiantai, Zhejiang, China

A primary school with a rooftop running track solves land shortage issues and adds functionality to an old city.

The project for the TianTai No. 2 Primary School strives for a unique design that will serve as a model school providing a beautiful environment for the cultivation of knowledge, culture, physical fitness, art, and ethics for elementary school children. The 200-meter running track called for 40 percent of the usable land if placed on the ground, resulting in a cramped campus space. Thus, the 200-meter running track was projected onto the roof level, giving an additional 32,290 square feet of usable area on the ground as well as the oval shape of the school building, which fosters a sense of inwardness and security for the students. In order to create more available green courtyard spaces, the building is twisted by approximately 15 degrees, creating smaller pockets of space between the site wall and the exterior envelope.

The rooftop track has three layers of guardrail to guarantee the safety of students. The exterior layer is a six-foot-high tempered glass wall, the middle layer is a 20-inch-wide green belt, and the interior layer is a four-foot-high stainless steel guardrail. For noise control, spring cushions are placed intermittently under the plastic track, thus reducing the kinetic noise by means of the double-layer structure.

Status
Built

Year
2014

Firm
LYCS Architecture

Firm location
Hangzhou, Zhejiang, China

Melgaço Sports School, IPVC Melgaço, Portugal

The new Melgaço Sports School provides a serene and integrated learning experience within the dynamic nature of a sports campus.

Located on the outskirts of the ancient village of Melgaço, the new Sports University Building offers a serene and integrated learning atmosphere in the dynamic atmosphere of the new Sports Campus.

As a result of an open public competition launched in 2008 by the Melgaço Municipality and the Viana do Castelo Polytechnic Institute, the building was conceived as a central hub for the High Performance Sports Campus, incorporating all administrative, educational, and social activities.

Based on a simple and clearly articulated geometric composition, the design strategy was a direct response to the challenges created by an imposing topography and a limited budget.

The design clearly distinguished between the social and administrative areas of the program in the anchored concrete volume, and the main educational areas located on the lighter, upper white volume.

The interaction between the building and the surrounding landscape also followed this strategy by clearly intensifying a direct and transparent relation between the main social areas, with large glass areas connected with the scenic countryside.

The design aimed to achieve a naturally balanced sustainable building, combining consistent passive design solutions, like the extensive use of natural lighting and ventilation, with the use of appropriate and long-lasting materials.

Status
Built

Year
2014

Firm
Pedro Reis Arquitecto

Firm location
Lisbon, Portugal

Melbourne School of Design Parkville, VIC, Australia

An innovative school of architecture with a hybrid atrium learning space and suspended visiting critics studio.

The University of Melbourne's new Faculty of Architecture, Building & Planning embraces the notion that the studio is not only a room or a space, but a way of learning that favors the acts of doing, making, and problem solving in a critical yet collaborative environment. In this definition the entire building has become the studio, incorporating two lecture theaters, a workshop, library, two exhibition spaces, a café, and a series of studios and associated academic and professional workspaces in the Studio Hall.

The Studio Hall is a large flexible space that provides for informal occupation throughout the day. The Studio Hall is enclosed by a continuous, coffered timber roof that suspends the visiting critics studio. Externally, the new building continues the sequence of outdoor rooms arrayed across the campus. Internally, the circulation occurs through a unique set of condensed stairs that allows the user to choose alternate routes through a Piranesian lacing of pathways and unusually wide corridors, which provide workspaces and exposure to other students' work.

The new building incorporates and combines a number of innovative structural, electrical, and climate systems with a high performance envelope, achieving the 6-star Green Star rating, an Australian equivalent of LEED.

Status
Built

Year
2014

Firm
NADAAA John Wardle Architects

Firm location
Boston, MA, USA

The City of the Books Mexico City, Mexico

An historic library reorganizes for a more logical and efficient operation.

'La Ciudadela' is a building from the end of the 18th century and was conceived as the Royal Tobacco Factory for Spain. It was built at the border of the colonial city of Mexico City and it has had different functions over time, including serving as a military headquarters, a prison, a weapons factory, a school, and from 1946 to the present, as a library. It was the first library in Mexico. In 1987, the building had a big intervention, designed by Abraham Zabludovsky, in which the four main patios and the central patio were covered with umbrella-like structures.

The new renovation aims to: a) recover the character of the building by taking back the functioning of the original patios and restoring the pathways crossing from north to south and in the perimeter of the building; b) improve the conditions of natural light and ventilation to get a better and more rational use of the energy and resources available; c) attend to the requirements of accessibility by using tactile guides, signals, and ramps in a topography that eliminates any kind of step in the common areas; and d) update the installations and equipment of the library according to the needs and uses of modern life.

Status
Built

Year
2013

Firm
bgp arquitectura

Firm location
**Mexico City,
Mexico**

James B. Hunt Jr. Library Raleigh, NC, USA

With collaborative spaces and technology, Hunt Library changes the concept of what a higher education library can be.

To support new modes of research, emerging technologies, and specific areas of faculty research excellence, the North Carolina State University James B. Hunt Jr. Library was envisioned as a technology sandbox for a campus already actively engaged in large-scale data and visualization, interactive computing, remote collaborations, and creative media production.

Embedded in the concept is the vision of a building dedicated to ongoing innovation across disciplinary boundaries. The result is a sustainable, social, and intellectual heart for the University's rapidly growing campus.

LEED Silver certified, the 230,000-square-foot facility is designed to provide an abundance of natural light and expansive views of nearby Lake Raleigh. The building's facade helps reduce heat gain while maximizing views and ambient natural light through the use of fritted glass and a fixed external aluminum shading system.

The library offers 30,000 books on open shelving, but an Automated Book Delivery System (ABDS), or bookBot, provides an efficient way to store up to two million items with a five-minute delivery time. Open spaces connect all floors of the library and invite exploration by moving up connecting stairs that lead to interactive social areas, technology-focused experimental labs, and adjacent private study rooms. Learning spaces with colorful, dynamic furnishings exist beside more traditional study rooms.

Status
Built

Year
2013

Firm
Clark Nexsen/ Snøhetta

Firm location
Virginia Beach, VA, USA

Court of Justice Hasselt, Belgium

A courthouse with courtrooms, offices, a cafeteria, and a library, located in the railway station area of Hasselt, Belgium.

The Court of Justice is one of two iconic projects within the new urban development around the main railway station in Hasselt, Belgium. The logistics and siting of the courthouse required multiple security barriers in a massing composed of three interconnected volumes. References include the old industrial steel structures that formerly occupied and defined the site, as well as the Belgian Art Nouveau forms constituting part of the cultural heritage of Hasselt.

There are also echoes of a tree, which is the Hasselt town emblem. The traces of the emblematic tree incorporated into the courthouse design also references the pre-medieval European tradition of holding a special 'place of speaking justice' underneath a large tree in the center of a town space.

Status
Built

Year
2013

Firm
**J. MAYER H.
Architects**

Firm location
Berlin, Germany

Knowledge Ship Rio de Janeiro, Brazil

Knowledge Ship: An architectural object that signals the future of a country with less social inequality through digital inclusion.

In Brazilian metropolitan areas, with much of its population living in deprived conditions, many young people drop out of school and are drawn to the street life and its violence. Social inequality in Brazil excludes the majority of its poor population from internet connection. To reverse this scenario, the city of Rio de Janeiro began the project Knowledge Ships in poorer areas of the city. With five initial units, the project aims to provide cutting-edge technology, entertainment, and educational projects. Its sustainable architectural concept reveals in its technological and poetic aesthetic the content of its political and educational agenda.

The design concept came from the image of an object floating in space, an elliptical ship reproducing the shape of the universe, hanging from the ceiling by rods. On a different plane, a glass wall limits the external and internal area of the building. The project's 4,305 square feet of space includes a study area, digital library, classroom, workshop space, digital gallery, and open cinema.

In its two years of existence, the success of the Knowledge Ship can be measured by more than one million visitors and approximately 9,000 students trained in its various workshops in Information, Communication, and Technology.

Status
Built

Year
2012

Firm
RioUrbe

Firm location
Rio de Janeiro, Brazil

Tongva Park and Ken Genser Square Santa Monica, CA, USA

Tongva Park reflects the identity of the city and creates a destination of great social, ecological, and symbolic value.

Situated on 7.4 acres between City Hall, the I-10 freeway, and Santa Monica's iconic palm tree lined Ocean Avenue, Tongva Park and Ken Genser Square have transformed a derelict and flat parking lot into a lush landscape of rolling hills, swales, Mediterranean meadow gardens, and active urban spaces.

Design and sustainability come together in this project to produce a new type of urban landscape that is active, innovative, resource-conscious, and ecologically rich. Shaped by extensive public participation, the design redefines the center of Santa Monica, reconnects the city fabric, and features a dynamic topography of rolling hills, meadows, and gardens. The project's sustainability is boldly evident not only in its ecology, use of water, energy, and materials, but also in its social vibrancy.

Inspired by the Southern California arroyo landscape, a series of braided pathways emerge from the footsteps of City Hall, extend west to Ocean Avenue and weave the park into the fabric of the city. Water and architectural features, a rich material palette, and lush planting reinforce the site's arroyo history and create an identity unique to Santa Monica. Dramatic topography reinforces the fluid pathway system and organizes the site into four thematic areas: Garden Hill, Discovery Hill, Observation Hill, and Gathering Hill.

Status
Built

Year
2014

Firm
**James Corner
Field Operations**

Firm location
New York, NY, USA

High Line at the Rail Yards New York, NY, USA

An elevated railway reclaimed as an extraordinary public space in the heart of Manhattan's West Side.

Representing one third of the High Line, the recently opened final section at the Rail Yards is one of the most iconic stretches of the High Line with expansive views of the Hudson River and the Midtown skyline. Section 3 builds upon the identity of the High Line, yet finds new ways to respond to the radically new 21st-century context of the future Hudson Yards development.

The design takes advantage of the east-west orientation to the river, respects the existing wild landscape and industrial aesthetic, and introduces the next iteration of design elements. These elements include new varieties of peel-up benches, a series of Rail Track Walks and tree groves that encourage users to walk along and within the train tracks, a bridge over 11th Avenue with heightened views of the River, and a unique children's play space. At the Western Rail Yards, a temporary walkway is placed over the existing, self-seeded landscape with large-scale furniture at key locations and dramatic views of the Hudson River. This latter section along the Western Rail Yards and 12th Avenue is perhaps the most subtle design, where the original High Line landscape, with its self-sown grasses and flowers emerging from old tracks, wood ties, and stone ballast, remains intact.

Status
Built

Year
2014

Firm
James Corner Field Operations (Project Lead) with Diller, Scofidio + Renfro and Piet Oudolf

Firm location
New York, NY, USA

The Painterly Approach Tiburon, CA, USA

A hillside garden solves a serious storm water management challenge while extending the usable space in the property.

Panoramic bay views drew the client to this family home on a steep hillside bordering a public open space of sweeping grassland. During initial construction of the house, the building foundation wall was improperly waterproofed and the cross slope was graded ineffectively, which resulted in extensive damage to the lower level of the house. Years later when the damage was discovered, the landscape architecture studio was brought in to correct the drainage issue, protect the repaired foundation, and create usable space for the family.

    The design sculpts the land to address both the drainage issue and create a reason for the family to be drawn to use this portion of the property. The design team devised a sinuous swale that winds down the slope, cutting the cross flow toward the house, and created an opportunity for a romantic, meandering pathway to an informal sitting area on the way to the pool area.

    The client wanted to honor the land and the habitat it provides. Thus, all plantings are deer tolerant, eliminating the need for a fence and allowing an uninterrupted connection to the grasslands. Many of the plantings are native to California, and all are low-water and drought-resistant.

Status
Built

Year
2012

Firm
Arterra Landscape Architects

Firm location
San Francisco, CA, USA

Riverpark Farm New York, NY, United States

An uncommon oasis, the 15,000-square-foot Riverpark Farm joins a growing movement in urban agriculture.

An uncommon oasis, the 15,000-square-foot Riverpark Farm joins a growing movement in urban agriculture, using unconventional spaces and technologies for crop harvesting within a densely populated environment. Riverpark restaurant owners approached ORE with the challenge of creating a farm at 29th Street and 1st Avenue in Manhattan to provide their kitchen with fresh produce.

The location, a stalled construction site adjacent to the restaurant, would be available until construction resumes on a new tower. It was thereby determined it would be crucial for the farm to be portable.

ORE's design uses cubic-foot milk crates as individual planters, keeping weight low and planting density high so all 3,000 plants can be moved in one day. The milk crates are lined with landscape fabric and filled with top soil, peat moss, and perlite soil, creating an air pocket that allows for air and water transfer with limited soil erosion. The modular nature of the milk crate also affords simple soil replacement, maximizing the efficiency of the farm as a whole.

The mobile design allowed for planting before the project's construction began. ORE sourced all the farm's materials from local growers and manufacturers. ORE also designed a dining area that is integrated into the farm.

Status
Built

Year
2011

Firm
ORE Design + Technology

Firm location
Brooklyn, NY, USA

The Big U New York, NY, USA

The BIG U is a 10-mile protective ribbon around lower Manhattan, consisting of multiple linked design opportunities.

Rebuild by Design addresses vulnerabilities exposed by Superstorm Sandy. The Big U is a vision for a 10-mile protective ribbon around lower Manhattan consisting of multiple linked design opportunities, with each local neighborhood tailoring its own set of programs, functions, and opportunities.

The US Department of Housing and Urban Development awarded The Big U $335 million in federal funding for the first phase, the Lower East Side (Compartment 1).

The Big U consists of 3 components: Big Bench, Battery Berm, and Berm. Big Bench is a continuous protective element adapted to local context that mediates new and existing infrastructure. It is designed like street furniture. Battery Berm weaves an elevated path through the park, enhancing the public realm while protecting the Financial District and critical transportation infrastructure beyond. This signature building will feature a structure which enables visitors to observe tidal variations and sea level rise while providing a flood barrier. The Berm rises 14 feet by the highways, connecting coast and community with greenways. Ultimately, the Berm will cap the highway.

The Big U serves as a new template for integrating resiliency with city-making. The floodplain behind the 10 miles of coastline is home to approximately 220,000 people and contains some of the largest business districts in the country, influencing economic activity globally.

Status
In Progress

Year
2014

Firm
BIG Team

Firm location
New York, NY, USA

A Gateway to Petra Wadi Musa, Petra, Jordan

A gateway that welcomes visitors from the dense urban setting of Wadi Musa to the serene journey into Petra.

Carved into sandstone of magnificent red hues and nestled amongst cliffs over 328 feet high, sits the prehistoric city of Petra. As Jordan's most valued touristic site, the Tourism Authority required a gate that streamlines the movement of visitors into and out of Petra.

While exploring the gate into Petra, it became apparent that a more comprehensive approach to the entire Wadi Musa entrance area was needed. The solution integrates the visitor center, the existing hotel, and the proposed museum. The design also embraces the current activities on the site, such as the kiosks, into a coherent urban solution. The aim is to create a design solution with minimal disruption to the natural topography.

The construction also uses local stone and building techniques, creating opportunities for local involvement in the project and enhancing social sustainability. The design scheme is about revitalizing the Wadi and creating gathering spaces. The design heightens one's awareness of past and present contexts, while providing a relevant architectural intervention. The project also seeks to minimize the negative environmental impact on such a sensitive urban context. Finally, the architectural approach consciously enables a sustainable and prosperous future for Petra and the generations of Wadi Musa.

Status
Built

Year
2013

Firm
maisam architects

Firm location
Amman, Jordan

Chhatrapati Shivaji Internatonal Airport, Terminal 2 Mumbai, India

Mumbai's new 4.4 million-square-foot integrated terminal building serves over 40 million passengers per year.

Located in the heart of India's financial capital, the new hub adds 4.4 million square feet of space to accommodate 40 million passengers per year, nearly twice as many as the building it replaces. By orchestrating the complex web of passengers and planes into a design that feels intuitive and responds to the region's rocketing growth, the new Terminal 2 asserts the airport's place as a preeminent gateway to India.

The new terminal combines international and domestic passenger services under one roof, optimizing terminal operations and reducing passenger walking distances. Inspired by the form of traditional Indian pavilions, the four-story terminal stacks a grand 'headhouse,' or central processing podium, on top of highly adaptable concourses below. The primary design feature of the building is a long-span roof covering various functional requirements, making it one of the largest roofs in the world without an expansion joint.

Just as the terminal celebrates a new global, high-tech identity for Mumbai, the structure is imbued with responses to the local setting, history, and culture. Gracious curbside drop-off zones designed for large parties accommodate traditional Indian arrival and departure ceremonies. Regional patterns and textures are also integrated into the terminal's architecture.

Status
Built

Year
2014

Firm
Skidmore, Owings & Merrill

Firm location
New York, NY, USA

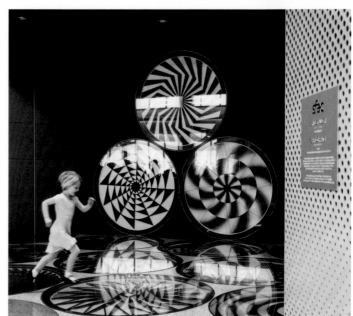

San Francisco International Airport, Boarding Area E
San Francisco, CA, USA

The renovated Terminal 3 Boarding Area E showcases innovative design, interactive technology, and a healthy environment.

Gensler's design for San Francisco International Airport's renovated Terminal 3 Boarding Area E (T3BAE) showcases innovative design, interactive technology, and a healthy environment carefully tuned to offer travelers a place where they will enjoy spending time. The 65,000-square-foot renovation features progressive sustainability measures that promote wellbeing, and is LEED-Gold certified.

A raised 'Flight Deck' interactive experience serves as an exciting physical point of entry to Boarding Area E, which includes 10 gates serving United Airlines. Highlighting service, hospitality, and comfort, T3BAE's design offers travelers many choices for how they would like to enjoy their time in the airport. Passengers can view the exquisite art, change clothes in private dressing rooms, stretch out in the Yoga Room, or let their children unwind in an interactive play area.

The project was built in a design-build partnership between Hensel Phelps and Gensler for San Francisco International Airport.

Status
Built

Year
2014

Firm
Gensler

Firm location
**San Francisco,
CA, USA**

Highway Rest Stops Highway Lochini, Georgia

Rest stops for a new highway in Lochini, Georgia.

In 2009 the head of the Roads Department of Georgia commissioned J. MAYER H. to design a system of 20 rest stops for the new highway, a thoroughfare that will run through Georgia and serve as a connection between the Republic of Azerbaijan and the Republic of Turkey. Two of the rest stops were completed in 2011 near Gori, and a third was finished in Lochini in 2012.

The new rest stops are located on selected scenic viewpoints along the route, and serve as economic and cultural facilitators for the surrounding area and neighboring cities. The rest stops aim to draw attention to nearby gas stations and supermarkets, as well as farmers' markets and a space for local arts and crafts.

Status
Built

Year
2012

Firm
**J. MAYER H.
Architects**

Firm location
Berlin, Germany

BRT Station Belo Horizonte, Brazil

A Bus Rapid Transit station project that merges with the urban landscape.

Contemporaneity and functionality, both harmoniously matching the urban landscape, were the guidelines for this BRT (Bus Rapid Transit) station project.

The shape of the station module aims at blending itself with the dynamic landscape. The modular stations, conceived in metallic structures, arrives at the construction site already pre-built, which allows for swiftness in construction and a high quality final product. The finish in ACM (Aluminum Composite Material) is another component that brings efficiency to the project, which can be replicated in other parts of the city and other regions of the country.

Access control to the station is made possible by the use of turnstiles, and is designed with disabled users in mind. The BRT system also offers comfort, making use of glass and perforated plates to enclose the sides, allowing for better visibility, lighting, and natural ventilation.

The equipment also covers the needs for sustainability and accessibility, which are concepts currently important to the population. Economical both in construction and maintenance, it has a system that allows for better use of internal ventilation and lighting, while also being fully accessible, welcoming cyclists, and promoting integration with other urban means of transportation.

Status
Built

Year
2014

Firm
GPA&A

Firm location
**Belo Horizonte,
Brazil**

Velenje Car Park Velenje, Slovenia

A parking area blends with the natural environment of the 1950s modernist garden city.

Velenje was designed in the 1950s as a garden city, and as a result the city has many unoccupied ground-level surfaces. The parking lot was originally intended to expand into the surrounding green surfaces due to insufficient capacity. Instead, we chose to partially dig in and cover the parking area, doubling the capacity in a simple way. As other projects in the area have shown, the abundance of space in the city made the users reluctant to adopt multi-level parking. Accordingly, the new parking lot is not designed as a classical parking garage but features a double entrance leading to two parking lots laid on top of each other.

The slight branching out in the floor area design reflects the sitting of the building among the existing trees, which have all been left intact. Individual facade panels are bent out of the building plane. Besides the interesting shape this strategy achieves, it also results in great static strength, which obviates the need for any additional support. The repetition and careful arrangement of these lightweight facade elements produces a constant play of light and shadow, giving the building a soft appearance among the surrounding trees.

Status
Built

Year
2014

Firm
ENOTA

Firm location
Ljubljana, Slovenia

The Z Detroit, MI, USA

The Z is an atypical parking experience and a mixed-use structure that changes the energy of Detroit.

Beginning as two surface lots on a single city block, The Z is a transformative mixed-use structure in Detroit's historic Broadway district.

The design team was tasked with creating a building in an area that needed more parking to attract young, vibrant talent returning to the city for work and entertainment. Responding to this need, The Z is a 10-level structure containing a 1,282-car garage with 33,000 square feet of ground-level retail and restaurant space.

White cement and aggregate precast concrete with a bold geometric 'picture frame' design is intended to reduce the scale of the 10-story structure. Its precast facade utilizes repetitive formwork to create faceted 'picture frame' panels and shear walls.

The Library Street Collective collaborated with the owner to bring in 27 urban muralists to beautify the inside of the parking garage. To create a 'museum' within its walls, murals are splashed on each of the 10 floors. A unique experience, the deck has already become an iconic destination for art tours and out-of-towners.

Spanning a public alley, the structure allows users to enter and exit onto two major arteries into and out of the city. The alley supports existing neighboring galleries, restaurants, and future tenants.

Status
Built

Year
2014

Firm
Neumann/Smith Architecture

Firm location
Southfield, MI, USA

Cykelslangen Copenhagen, Denmark

'The bicycle snake' project in Copenhagen is a long orange bridge meandering over the harbor.

In 2011 the City of Copenhagen published its planning strategy for becoming the world's best bicycle city by 2015.

Already in 2010 a series of initiatives were taken. Amongst these initiatives was a general consultant tender for a bicycle ramp to complete a path across the Copenhagen Harbor from Islands Brygge to Kalvebod Brygge, of which the first stage, the Brygge Bridge, was already in use. The cyclists were left with a rundown staircase to take them up 18 feet to Kalvebod Brygge Street.

Our design aimed to unfold the ramp, curve it across the water, and in between buildings, and down close to the Brygge Bridge. The results would achieve a clear pathway that was more joyful to ride on, with gentler gradients and better curvature.

The project went from a ramp to an elevated bicycle route. The vibrant color orange gives the structure a unique place amidst the surroundings, as well as a sense of warmth at night.

The bridge is carried by a central steel spine—an airtight welded steel box girder—from which a series of struts carry the steel plate deck. The design strives for transparency, simplicity, and structural refinement. The parapet is also conceived as a transparent film, underlining the fluidity of movement through space.

Status
Built

Year
2014

Firm
DISSING+ WEITLING

Firm location
Copenhagen, Denmark

Tabiat Pedestrian Bridge Tehran, Iran

Connecting two public parks, this curvy pedestrian bridge is designed to be a place to linger rather than to pass through.

Tabiat Bridge was designed to improve access for pedestrians between two public parks divided by highways. Instead of connecting two points to each other, the idea was to create multiple paths in each park that would lead people to the bridge.

This bridge is a place to linger rather than to pass through; there are seating areas and green spaces on all parts of the bridge, as well as restaurants on both sides of the lower level. The curved path with variable widths and changes in slopes slows down the users and creates a sense of mystery about the destination.

Since the site was covered by trees, the number and location of columns were designed in a way to have a minimal footprint on the ground to avoid having to remove trees. The structural concept is a dynamic 3D truss with two continuous deck levels that sit on three columns. The point at which the truss meets the columns is the highest and widest juncture, where the bridge becomes three levels. This area acts as a viewing platform. All the levels are connected to each other by stairs and ramps, providing multiple paths throughout the bridge from one level to another.

Status
Built

Year
2014

Firm
Diba Tensile Architecture

Firm location
Tehran, Iran

Fujiko Nakaya: Veil New Canaan, CT, USA

Fujiko Nakaya: "A veil at the glass house."

The Glass House presents "Fujiko Nakaya: Veil," the first site-specific artist installation to engage Philip Johnson's iconic Glass House itself since its completion in 1949. Nakaya, a Japanese artist who has produced fog sculptures and environments internationally, enshrouds the Glass House in a dense, periodic fog. For approximately ten minutes each hour, the Glass House appears to vanish, only to return as the mist dissipates. Inside the structure, the sense of being outdoors is temporarily suspended during misty weather. "Veil" establishes a potent dialogue with the Glass House by producing an opaque enclosure that complements the building's radical transparency, reaffirming its overall timelessness.

   Situated on a promontory overlooking a valley, the Glass House is subject to changing wind patterns, as well as variable temperature and humidity, which will continually influence the interchange between "Veil" and the building it obscures. Fresh water, pumped at high pressure through 600 nozzles, will produce an immersive environment that reveals these dynamic conditions.

Status
Built

Year
2014

Firm
The Glass House

Firm location
New Canaan, CT, USA

MINI Brand Experience Centre Shanghai, China

The building as a 'walkable sculpture' and an incarnation of MINI brand values: urban, dense, complex, and not normal!

The MINI Brand Experience Centre is the first of its kind worldwide, and opened at the prominent location of the former EXPO site in Shanghai.

The design refers to the main codes of the MINI brand architecture and follows a rectangular grid system in all three dimensions. The Centre is black in appearance and accentuated with illuminated color frames.

The building is a 52-foot-high 'walkable sculpture' consisting of a steel frame with three attached boxes, carrying the different floor functions with individual themes. 'Be MINI. A MINI WELCOME' is on the ground floor, which is open and articulates the entrance. 'THE WORLD OF MINI' is on the second floor, which accommodates the showroom with two cars. 'MINIFY YOUR LIFE' is on the third floor, containing a lifestyle space. And finally, 'MINI UNITED LOUNGE' is on the fourth floor, offering a bar and seating lounge as well as the best view to the China Pavilion.

Every box is shifted in a different direction in order to differentiate the floors from each other. The different floors are accessed via an outdoor staircase that exhibits additional MINI analog communication.

The verticality is not only eye catching, but also creates density inside and challenges the expectations a visitor might have for the space.

Status
Built

Year
2013

Firm
BMW China, Architectural Design Team

Firm location
Beijing, China

Airbnb Portland Office Portland, OR, USA

Airbnb's Portland office revolutionizes work by creating a space that invites employees to 'belong anywhere.'

Airbnb's Portland office revolutionizes work by creating a space that invites employees to 'belong anywhere.' The design dissolves the idea of a desk as an individual's address at work. The desk is replaced with the spatially efficient 'landing spot,' a veritable Swiss Army Knife of storage/workspace/team identity. From here the office is a landscape of shared amenities, including comfy lounges, communal tables, standing monitor stations, even a tree house.

Seventy percent of the furniture is locally fabricated, custom built for the CX workflow. It took an unorthodox project team to bring this to life in under 8 months; both in the architect/designer relationship and with the local Airbnb employees.

Rather than hiring an interior design firm to build out the traditional Airbnb listing based conference rooms we led the local Airbnb employees in a two-month design workshop. Thirteen teams of five conceptualized, shopped, and installed each of the conference room interiors. The resulting spaces are unique worlds within the office that earned a deep level of employee engagement with the new space.

Boora Architects' expertise in workplace design and local knowledge made them a great partner to execute this innovative project in a compressed timeline without sacrificing quality or detail.

Status
Built

Year
2015

Firm
Airbnb

Firm location
San Francisco, CA, USA

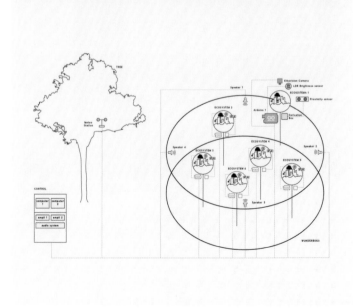

Wunderbugs Rome, Italy

Wunderbugs is an interactive pavilion with sensors collecting environmental changes, allowing insects to modulate music.

Wunderbugs is made possible thanks to the cooperation of several experts who have created the perfect design field through a synergy of architecture and other disciplines. It involves architects, narrators, musicians, sound engineers, biologists, insect farmers, carpenters, and behavior specialists.

Wunderbugs is a wooden pavilion combining traditional techniques and computer-numerical control machines. Inspired by the typical shapes of the Roman Baroque, and hybridized with geometries that the insects are capable of producing, the pavilion was seen as an aggregation of repetitive and simple elements.

Wunderbugs can assume infinite configurations thanks to its modularity realized through the careful combination of 1,104 arc modules, 92 rhombuses which adjust the pavilion's fullness or emptiness, and 198 knobs in wood that regulate the curvilinear progress. Its six spherical interactive ecosystems are equipped with Arduino and sensors for motion, humidity, temperature, and intensity of sunlight. This data, combined with the information collected by a network of ultrasonic sensors able to detect the position of the visitors, is used to modulate in real time the Wunderbugs musical composition.

Status
Built

Year
2014

Firm
OFL Architecture

Firm location
Rome, Italy

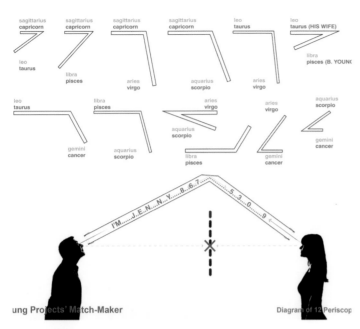

sagittarius **capricorn** sagittarius **capricorn** sagittarius **capricorn** sagittarius **capricorn** leo **taurus** leo **taurus (HIS WIFE)**

leo **taurus** libra **pisces** aries **virgo** aquarius **scorpio** aries **virgo** libra **pisces (B. YOUNG**

leo **taurus** libra **pisces** aries **virgo** aquarius **scorpio**

gemini **cancer** aquarius **scorpio** aquarius **scorpio** libra **pisces** gemini **cancer** gemini **cancer**

I'M.....J.E.N..N..Y......8..6..7...........5..3..0......9

...ung Projects' Match-Maker   Diagram of 12 Periscop

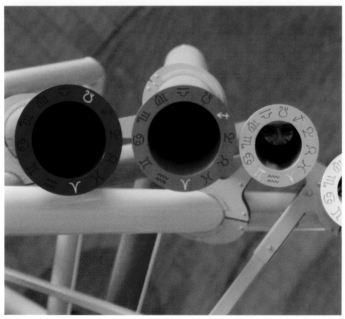

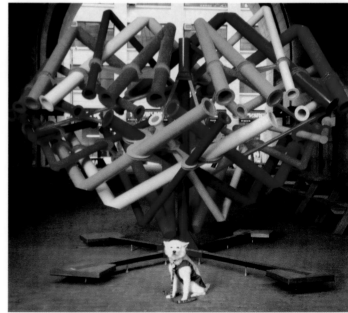

Match-Maker: 2014 Times Square Valentine Heart New York, NY, USA

The Match-Maker Heart promotes the visceral experience of analog communication through tangled tunnels of love.

As social media and online profiles propagate alter egos, we suggest a momentary diversion from looking to one's mobile device for connection; instead, we encourage the public to communicate with those within their immediate context. In this regard, Match-Maker—the winning pavilion for the 2014 Times Square Valentine Heart (Times Square Arts/Van Alen Institute)—is both radical and urgent as an architectural solution that directly engages communication as an integral design parameter.

Guided by their zodiac sign and iconography developed in collaboration with graphic designer Dungjai, visitors arrange themselves at twelve points around the heart-shaped sculpture. Peering through colorful, interwoven periscopes provides glimpses of each viewer's four most ideal astrological mates, offering novel visual and auditory connections. From many points of view the sculpture forms a perfect and iconic heart, from other perspectives it is tangled and perplexing.

The modest scale of the pavilion fosters a sense of physical proximity, yet the carefully arranged standing positions simultaneously offers a sense of protected anonymity. This analog means of communication responds to the near-ubiquity of digital technologies as the primary driver for creating new connections. In contrast, the strongest evidence of Match-Maker's relevance is apparent in the faces of the pavilion's visitors.

Status
Built

Year
2014

Firm
Young Projects
Kammetal

Firm location
Brooklyn, NY, USA

Women's Opportunity Center Kayonza, Rwanda

The Women's Opportunity Center empowers women to transcend a legacy of conflict, as well as creating an ethic of global collaboration.

The Women's Opportunity Center (WOC), designed in collaboration with Women for Women International, occupies a two-hectare site one hour from the Rwandan capital. WOC has been developed with the following objectives in mind: to empower its community, create economic opportunity, and rebuild social infrastructure.

Referencing a Rwandan village, we clustered pavilions to create security and cultivate the sense of community. Facilities include classrooms, guest lodgings, a demonstration farm cooled by green roof and retained earth walls, and a marketplace where women sell products that they have made onsite. As well as designing innovative buildings that allow passive cooling and solar shading, we established local partnerships to create water purification, biogas, and other sustainable systems that can be maintained by the site's inhabitants.

The 450,000 clay bricks needed for the construction were made at the center by local women, using a durable manual press method which we adapted from local building techniques. As a result, women have learned marketable, income-generating skills and are now being hired as masons in the area.

A further and integral objective of WOC was to involve as many stakeholders as possible, with recognition of the value of partnerships and community-based knowledge, especially within a region where resources are scarce.

Status
Built

Year
2013

Firm
Sharon Davis Design

Firm location
New York, NY, USA

Glacier Skywalk Jasper National Park, Alberta, Canada

The Glacier Skywalk is an extension of the landscape, projecting from the mountain slope to educate, expose, and astound.

The Glacier Skywalk, designed by Sturgess Architecture and structural consultant Read Jones Christofferson, was completed for CAD $18 million in May 2014. Located in the heart of the Canadian Rockies overlooking the Columbia ice fields, the project consists of a 1,475-foot walkway integrated into the mountainside, ending in a gravity-defying viewing platform projected out from the cliff face.

The walkway is one of discovery and surprise, hiding and exposing the outlook through carefully orchestrated interpretive stations along the way. At the climax of the trail, the steel outlook extends 115 feet from the mountainside culminating in a glass floor viewing platform.

The elegant engineering behind this feat begins with the structure's naturally sturdy parabolic shape, which allows the use of a unique cable suspension system to minimize visible support and enhance the sense of exposure experienced by visitors. The glass walkway is supported by steel tubes that were bent in three dimensions and contain the same type of cables used in a large cable-stayed bridge.

The thrust-fault geological movement and the resulting fractal landscape informed the larger formal gesture of the architecture. The angular forms, rusted hues, and warm texture of the weathering steel finish are a nod to the rocky outcroppings of the mountain itself.

Status
Built

Year
2014

Firm
Sturgess Architecture

Firm location
Calgary, Alberta, Canada

Hello Wood International Architecture Camp Csórompuszta, Hungary

A camp that provides a unique opportunity for learning based on making.

Hello Wood started as an art camp in 2010 for students in architecture and design, and has grown into an international project involving more than 20 universities and 30 countries. The program welcomes 150 university students and young professionals yearly, from Sweden to the United States, who work in teams for 8 days. Teams are made of 6–8 students, mixing different forms of art, nationalities, and institutions, and led by experienced workshop leaders. A design concept is developed and realized through teamwork. We cooperate with several universities, including Moholy-Nagy University of Art and Design Budapest and TU Delft ot Angewandte Vienna. The results of the program are published internationally and can be seen by thousands of visitors of the Sziget Festival in Budapest where the installations are exhibited every year. Besides the university program, Hello Wood organizes architecture and design camps for children.

All work produced here carries two attributes: it is mostly from wood and it is characterized by an interplay of art and social commitment. Hello Wood believes that the camp can complement higher education by focusing on learning based on making, gaining unique types of knowledge in ways that are impossible in formal education. Making architecture itself is the key learning tool.

Status
Built

Year
2014

Firm
Hello Wood

Firm location
Budapest, Hungary

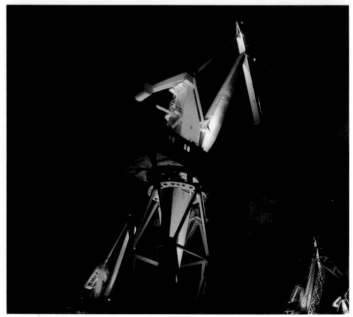

Shipyard Cranes—Lighting Giants Pula, Croatia

A lighting design project for active shipyard cranes.

The Mediterranean city of Pula is known for its shipyard Uljanik, one of the oldest working shipyards in the world. Uljanik, built in 1856, is the focal point of the city, and its majestic cranes are bathed in lights.

The project is a large-scale light feature adding a vertical axis to the sea, and creating a dynamic sculpture in the night landscape.

The eight cranes, with the capacity of 200, 150, and 45 tons, are functional as well as monumental. The shipyard is also active and continues to build ships, which makes this project unique in the world.

The lighting designers, engineers, and technicians illuminated the cranes with 73 RGB Colorcinetic LED spotlights, weighing 88 pounds each. Each light consists of 64 pieces of LED chips that can be programmed to 16,000 different variations of color and intensity. Different lighting effects can thus be adjusted for various occasions and celebrations.

This blend of technology and history is sensitive to the city's past as a shipyard harbor, celebrating the generations of workers that constituted the heart of Pula. The cranes continue to shine for fifteen minutes on every hour from 9 p.m. until midnight, giving the city of Pula a living sculpture.

Status
Built

Year
2014

Firm
Skira

Firm location
Pula, Croatia

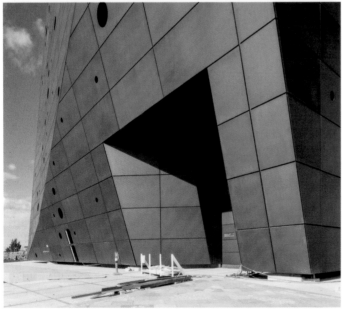

Incineration Line Roskilde, Denmark

Facade design for the new Incineration Line in Roskilde, Denmark.

The new Incineration Line will incinerate waste from nine surrounding municipalities and from many places abroad to produce electricity and heat for the whole region of Roskilde, Denmark. The design presents an iconic expression of the architecture of the local waste management company KARA/NOVEREN. The facade consists of two layers: the inner layer that provides the actual climatic barrier, and the outer facade. The facade has raw umber-colored aluminum plates with an irregular pattern of laser-cut circular holes. At night, the programmable lighting installed between the two facades gives the building an additional ambient tenor.

The illumination of the facade has been realized by reflecting the light on the inner facade, which allows the light to glow through the perforated skin. However, the lighting is not intended to brighten the sky or dominate the surroundings, but rather serves to underline the building's industrial character while also giving it a poetic experience.

The design is based on simple construction details combined with cutting edge manufacturing technology for the production of the aluminum facade panels. Due to its large scale, the incinerator is destined to become an outstanding structure in the Roskilde area, and represents a hypermodern and sustainable energy plant where waste is turned into power.

Status
Built

Year
2014

Firm
Erick van Egeraat

Firm location
**Rotterdam,
Netherlands**

House in Tamatsu Osaka, Japan

A residential house designed for a family with two children.

This residential project is situated in the urban area of Osaka, Japan, with a floor area of only 463 square feet. The surroundings consist of a varied, disjointed mix of small houses, small factories, and small office buildings. The adjacent buildings were too close to let natural light enter into the original house. Therefore, one of the crucial client requests was to make a family room as large as possible and bear no pillars or road-bearing walls, allowing natural light to freely enter the house.

Due to structural reasons, the large openings which faced the street could not be placed on the first floor of the building. As a result, the second floor's volume was rotated 14 degrees from the main building axis; thus, interstitial spaces between the rotated wall and the outer wall turned into voids. The skylight was positioned in the upper section of the void, allowing natural light to enter the family room in the first floor.

The white, box-shaped building is completely distinct from the buildings of the surrounding neighborhood. The interior has a simple yet charismatic character, including box-shaped, cantilevered stairs floating in the main void.

Status
Built

Year
2012

Firm
Ido,Kenji Architectural Studio

Firm location
Osaka, Japan

The Courtyard House Plugin Beijing, China

A prefabricated building system for inserting modern living conditions into dilapidated Chinese courtyard houses.

The Courtyard House Plugin is essentially a house within a house. It is a prefabricated modular system designed to bring modern living standards and energy efficiency to traditional Chinese courtyard houses that are centuries old. Today, old and dilapidated, the courtyards are vacated for newer housing in the suburbs. Because parts of these courtyards are still occupied by other families, any structural changes would affect their property.

The People's Architecture Office developed a new type of prefabricated panel that can be inserted into these old buildings while leaving the original structure untouched. The panels are made of a composite that incorporates structure, insulation, wiring, plumbing, windows, doors, interior, and exterior finishes into one molded part. They snap and lock together with the use of a single tool, a hex wrench. The entire Plugin structure can be assembled by a few people in one day, and requires no skill or special training.

In China, countless examples of 'historic preservation' projects are merely sanitized versions of old buildings that ignore and erase the traces of history. While these courtyards are historic structures, they are not museums frozen in time. The ambition of the Plugin is to renew interest in historic neighborhoods not as tourist destinations, but as places for living.

Status
Built

Year
2014

Firm
People's Architecture Office

Firm location
Beijing, China

Z53 Mexico City, Mexico

With the use of the single component of red mud artisanal brick, the designers produced a heterogeneous coherence for this housing project.

The project is located on a rectangular plot with its short side facing the street, in an area with a high demand for social housing in Mexico City. The 42 units are placed in three towers, generating interior courtyards for views and natural ventilation to each apartment, and connected with vertical cores and bridges above the patios.

The structure on the parking level is made of reinforced concrete, transferring the loads to masonry brick walls on the five levels above. The brick walls play an important role in the project as they are part of the structure and reinterpret the traditional brick wall, blurring the boundary between structure and ornament.

With the use of the single component of red mud artisanal brick, we were able to produce a heterogeneous coherence in the facades, creating walls that are sensitive to shadows and lights. The constraints of the project, such as budget, materials, structure, and density, were conceived as opportunities generating new spatial qualities that respond to the local aesthetic. These constraints also produced new alternatives and relationships between technology and tradition.

Status
Built

Year
2012

Firm
MAP/MX + GRUPO NODUS

Firm location
Mexico City, Mexico

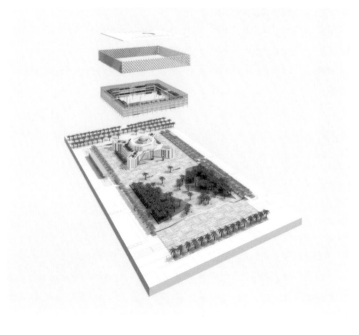

King Fahad National Library Riyadh, Saudi Arabia

The facade of the library reinterprets the Arabian tent structure in a more modern, technological way.

The King Fahad National Library is one of the most important cultural buildings in the Kingdom of Saudi Arabia. The design functions as the central driving force behind a piece of urban development, and combines the challenge of designing within the existing context and a respect for Arabian culture. The square new building, which encloses the old building, is covered by a lightweight textile facade following traditional Middle Eastern architectural patterns, as well as linking them with state-of-the-art technology.

The key element of the facade was developed especially for the new building. It is a cladding made up of lozenge-shaped textile awnings, which playfully reveals and conceals. White membranes, supported by a 3D, tensile-stressed steel cable structure, act as sunshades and reinterpret the Arabian tent structure tradition in a modern, technological way.

One particular challenge for the facade are the enormous temperature differences in Saudi Arabia. These effects had to be calculated to optimize the tension of the steel wires which expand in the hot temperatures. The facade was equipped with layered ventilation and floor cooling. In this way, thermal comfort was increased and energy consumption significantly reduced by using special methods and technologies for the first time in the Arab world.

Status
Built

Year
2013

Firm
Gerber Architekten

Firm location
Dortmund, Germany

One Main Boston, MA, USA

An office renovation utilizes subtle digital form, sustainable timber, and CNC machining.

This project was for the penthouse offices of an investment group in green building and clean energy technologies. The design intention was to propose the milling of all elements of the interior from sustainably forested spruce plywood using numeric command machines.

The project comprises two planes, the floor and ceiling, both of which are articulated as continuous surfaces inflected by function. The curvature expresses both the digital genesis and the seamless fabrication logic, with the architect providing actual machining files to the fabricator. The intention was to offer a reduced carbon footprint while celebrating both a new formal virtuosity and a radical level of detail finesse. This effect allows the architect to fully customize all elements of the building, placing material in space with full authorial control.

The entire project was nested onto 1,200 4-by-12-foot plywood sheets, and milled using a small 3-axis CNC router, which effortlessly carved the ply sections according to our prescribed tool paths. Over one million linear feet of cut were issued, yet the machine's process was essentially error-free and highly accurate. Assembly proved relatively straightforward given the accuracy of the milling, and we enjoyed the elegance of the emerging forms.

Status
Built

Year
2011

Firm
dECOi architects

Firm location
Boston, MA, USA

Sifang Art Museum Nanjing, China

A film to introduce viewers to the ethereal, spiritual experience of the Sifang Art Museum.

The Sifang Art Museum, designed by Steven Holl Architects, is a museum about parallax and the body's movement through space. Sited in the lush green landscape of the Pearl Spring near Nanjing, China, the site and courtyard are planned by strategically placed bamboo formed concrete walls that seem to crisscross in your path, forcing perspectives to change dramatically as you move toward the entrance of the museum. This mysterious feeling confounds your idea of a vanishing point and is directly inspired by the 13th-century Chinese paintings of parallel perspectives, in which the viewer travels with the painting. In contrast, as you enter the museum, the experience of the upper galleries is reversed. Fixed perspectives spiral you around the space and the curated artwork and culminate with the distant view of the city of Nanjing.

Holl says, "A place of reflection about art should be a place of reflection about the spiritual dimension of life," and this film introduces the viewers to this ethereal spiritual experience. Birds chirp in the silence of the landscape, the museum glows like a lantern on top of a hill, and perspectives challenge the existence of the very moment you are in.

Status
Built

Year
2014

Firm
Spirit Of Space

Firm location
Chicago, IL, USA

Seinäjoki Library Seinäjoki, Finland

Seinäjoki Library by JKMM Architects.

The city of Seinäjoki in central Finland is known as the most extensive cluster of buildings designed by Alvar Aalto in the world, including the old library. Completed as part of the civic center in 1965, the library was due for an expansion to meet modern-day needs.

Connected by an underground link, the new library stands separate from the old library. The building is divided into three units such that the large building volume blends into the surrounding city.

These images express the care and dedication with which the Seinäjoki Library was designed and built. Although it seems like a straightforward subject, the building was best captured not in a single photo shoot but over a longer timeframe, to properly give a sense the daily rhythm and character of the space.

Status
Built

Year
2012

Firm
Decopic

Firm location
Espoo, Finland

Guthrie Transportation Museum & Welcome Center Guthrie, KY, USA

The project rehabilitates two buildings in an advanced state of decay through a grass-roots community effort.

The city of Guthrie is a small rural community in southern Kentucky that once played a significant role in the expansion of the country's transportation network in the early 1900s through the construction of the Louisville and Nashville Railroad line. After a period of economic decline, the city has recently been the focus of renewal efforts to revive its downtown core. The project addresses several overlapping community interests:

- To structurally stabilize, preserve, and rehabilitate two historic brick storefront structures that were in an advanced state of decay and partial collapse.

- To create a facility to welcome visitors and share the story of Guthrie's role in the early development of the country's railroad industry.

- To provide a multi-use venue as a place for the community to gather.

The design process was guided by a collaborative team comprised of the entire community, the Kentucky Heritage Council, and state and federal agencies.

The design approach utilizes a simple strategy of three key elements: a new structural steel frame to stabilize the existing buildings, a 'black box' zone that consolidates core support functions in order to maximize open flexible spaces, and a new concrete service tower for vertical circulation that also functions as a structural anchor.

Status
Built

Year
2014

Firm
De Leon & Primmer Architecture Workshop

Firm location
Louisville, KY, USA

The Three Cusps Chalet Braga, Portugal

The "Three Cusps Chalet" combines 19th-century Portuguese architecture with an unexpected alpine influence from Brazil.

We wanted to go against a current tide of refurbishment projects that consist of the demolition of a historic building, while retaining a hollow facade in front of a contemporary construction.

The "Three Cusps Chalet" is a very peculiar building. It documents the region's history of diaspora, combining typical 19th-century Portuguese architecture and urban design with an alpine influence brought by an emigration wave of rich Portuguese returning from Brazil in the 1800s.

The building was conceived as an annex serving the small adjacent palace that sits at the heart of both the Roman and Medieval walls of Braga. It is a sunny building with two fronts, one facing the street to the west and the other facing a delightful block interior plaza to the east.

The building's identity has been lost over 120 years of small unqualified interventions closing it to the street and to the light. The facade was equally adulterated, including additions of modern aluminum window frames and exterior shade head boxes, changing the building's scale, detail, and original atmosphere.

The goal of this design was to clarify the building's spaces and functions, return the building to its original image, and simultaneously make it fit for today's way of living.

Status
Built

Year
2013

Firm
**Tiago do Vale
Arquitectos**

Firm location
Braga, Portugal

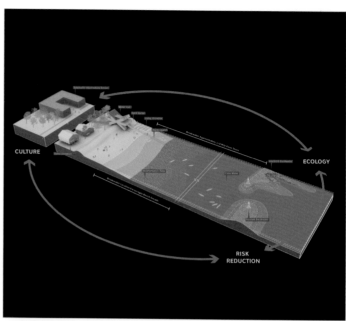

CULTURE

ECOLOGY

RISK
REDUCTION

SUPERLEVEE
DEVELOPMENT

RECREATION CENTER PROVIDES
AMENITIES FOR UNDERSERVED
COMMUNITIES

SOFTENED
EDGES BET
WETLAND &

COMMUNITY PROTECTION

Rebuild by Design New York, NY, USA

Rebuild by Design offers an innovative process for developing a more resilient future.

Rebuild by Design was created in response to the physical and social vulnerabilities uncovered by Hurricane Sandy. Supported by private philanthropy, partner organizations, and HUD, the design competition created a process that combined design thinking with cross-sector collaboration to develop implementable designs for regional resiliency. In 2014, HUD allocated $930 million to implement the first stages of the final proposals.

Ten interdisciplinary teams—including designers, engineers, architects, academics, climate experts, and others—undertook an iterative, cooperative process of design development. These teams held meetings with countless individuals, community organizations, and government agencies to gain an understanding of the complex social, infrastructural, economic, and ecological challenges.

These renderings represent the seven funded projects, comprehensive solutions to these problems based on the needs and experiences of local residents. Working with community members and experts, the teams tested and refined their proposals not only to address local problems but also to ensure that they could be replicated worldwide.

Status
Concept

Year
2022

Firm
Rebuild by Design

Firm location
New York, NY, USA

The Gourd San Antonio, TX, USA

A human-sized birdhouse, the Gourd is a testament to working for and with community.

A human-sized birdhouse built for the San Antonio Botanical Gardens, the Gourd is a testament to working for and with community, and offers a playful platform in which to contemplate the complex relationship between humans and the natural world.

Rather than pursuing a form that resembles a small human house as is typically seen in most manmade birdhouses, the design team chose a form inspired by the bottle gourd. The organic form inspires creativity and imagination, particularly in its youngest users, while pushing the limits of digital design and fabrication.

The Gourd is built out of 70 plates of 12GA Cor-ten steel that are wrapped around an internal octahedron structure, and perforated with over 1,000 Ball Mason jars. The jars illuminate the interior space while providing a visible connection to the outside world. Each steel plate, unique in shape and size, was fabricated using CNC laser cutting technology and emulates the pattern of a dragonfly wing.

Fabricated and assembled in house by the design team, the project provided young designers a firsthand education in material characteristics and craftsmanship. The project serves as an exemplar model of high-end digital fabrication and finely honed craft, bringing an experientially unexpected space to life for the local community.

Status
Built

Year
2012

Firm
Overland Partners

Firm location
San Antonio, TX, USA

Dixon Water Foundation Josey Pavilion Decatur, TX, USA

A fully restorative Living Building, the open-air Josey Pavilion represents the most advanced measure of sustainability.

With aspirations to be the first Living Building project in Texas, this 5,400-square-foot open-air pavilion is an education and meeting center that serves as a demonstration site for the Dixon Water Foundation.

The building's simple, low-lying forms speak to the surrounding native prairie as the pavilion works in concert with nature. The complex consists of two similarly scaled buildings connected by a shady porch; one includes a herbarium, restroom, and kitchen, while the other houses a multi-purpose space for education events. Designed to be flexible and adapt to climatic conditions year round, the structure captures cool breezes in summer and blocks cold winter winds.

The project represents the most advanced measure of sustainability in the built environment. 100 percent of wastewater is treated onsite and returned to the natural water cycle. At least 100 percent of the energy used is produced by solar panels and testing has confirmed that indoor air quality is almost indistinguishable from surrounding outdoor fresh air. Only building materials that have a low environmental impact and no adverse effects to human health were used in the entire project. Natural materials and human scaled spaces create a tranquil environment that connects people with the landscape in a holistic, non-intrusive way.

Status
Built

Year
2014

Firm
Lake|Flato Architects

Firm location
San Antonio, TX, USA

J. Craig Venter Institute La Jolla, CA, USA

The first net-zero energy biological laboratory in the United States.

This not-for-profit research Institute needed a west coast home and wanted the layout of the building to encourage interaction, while also addressing the Institute's ambitious sustainability goals. Designed to achieve LEED-Platinum certification and a net-zero energy footprint, the building is the first net-zero energy biological laboratory in the U.S.

The design solution includes a separate wet laboratory wing and a dry lab/office wing surrounding a central courtyard. Locating the office spaces and dry computational laboratories in one wing, and wet laboratories in the other, reduced energy loads and optimized the mechanical systems. The project uses a modest palette of materials, including high-performance glazing, high-strength concrete (with 30 percent fly ash), and Spanish cedar wood that will age naturally. Each material was considered for its contribution to the enhancement of the building's performance, resulting in a building that is both functional and artful in its simplicity.

Architecturally, the building is a metaphor for a ship: the wood is reminiscent of a sailing vessel and the building is self-sustaining and environmentally stable, powered by sun and water. The building was also oriented to maximize output from the rooftop solar arrays' 1,488 Sunpower E20/327 panels, predicted to exceed the building demand and take advantage of ocean views.

Status
Built

Year
2014

Firm
ZGF Architects

Firm location
Los Angeles, CA, USA

The Stack New York, NY, USA

The Stack finds opportunity to utilize offsite modular construction to develop housing on small, difficult urban sites.

The Stack is a pilot project for developing a quality and economically viable housing solution to strategically rebuilding outmoded housing infrastructure in the city. It utilizes offsite construction which offers an accelerated schedule and shorter financing period, turning sites that might otherwise be considered risky into opportunities.

Although not necessary to this construction methodology, the design of this 7-story residential building expresses its modular construction. Each individual modular unit is legible but also reads as part of a knit-together whole. A common misconception of modular construction is that the units are products, each one containing a complete apartment of a specific design. In fact, offsite construction is simply an alternate construction method. The building is designed according to its needs and then 'cut' into pieces that can be fabricated in the factory, and then transported to its intended location.

This project is the first prefabricated steel and concrete multi-unit residential building to be erected in New York City. The project consists of 28 apartments built with 56 complete factory-finished modules prefabricated offsite. The 5,000 square feet of infrastructure and foundations were built onsite, in the same first three months that 28,000 square feet of building were simultaneously assembled in the factory. A steel column grid structure was built on top of a concrete foundation to receive the stacked modules.

Status
Built

Year
2014

Firm
GLUCK+

Firm location
New York, NY, USA

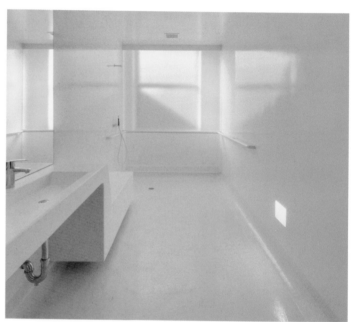

Red Bull New York Office New York, NY, USA

Red Bull's New York office space is focused on the experience of the basic architectural qualities of scale and light.

Best known for its high-energy drink, the company wanted its New York offices to be low key in atmosphere. The 16,800-square-foot project does not celebrate the company's values with eye-catching forms, nor is the layout inspired by recent theories of workplace productivity. Instead, the design is simple and without the pretense of being on the cutting edge of cool tech office design. It responds to the quick cycling of trends in workplace interiors by steering clear of large-scale gestures, playful lounge zones, or urban-inspired ad hoc decor.

Status
Built

Year
2014

Firm
INABA

Firm location
Brooklyn, NY, USA

The David & Lucille Packard Foundation Headquarters Los Altos, CA, USA

A new office building with passive, bio-climatic design strategies that support the core philanthropic mission of the client.

The new office building for The David and Lucile Packard Foundation was designed to serve as a catalyst for broader organizational sustainability initiatives by achieving net zero energy use and LEED Platinum certification. It is the largest building to date to received New Zero Energy Certification.

Two 40-foot-wide workplace modules were pulled apart to create an indigenously landscaped outdoor atrium which functions as the project's largest room and active meeting space most of the year. The program was organized around the atrium to allow for maximum transparency through the site by way of two glass bridges separating the wings which house collaboration spaces. The demarcation between indoors and outdoors is blurred with the help of sliding partitions at the atrium's ground-level perimeter.

Rainwater is collected for toilet flushing and irrigation, and storm water is retained on-site. Inside, meeting rooms are outfitted for remote collaboration, promising dramatic reductions in travel-related carbon emissions. Additionally, a transportation demand management plan helped eliminate the need for an $8 million underground parking garage, further reducing the organization's carbon footprint.

Through integrated building design and aggressive reductions in plug loads, the building's energy use was reduced by 65 percent. In addition, innovative use of roof-mounted photovoltaic panels offsets any energy use.

Status
Built

Year
2012

Firm
EHDD

Firm location
San Francisco, CA, USA

Jurors

Charles Adler	Co-Founder, Kickstarter
Sabah Al Abbasi	Chief Creative Consultant & Editor-in-Chief, Shawati
Faris Al-Shathir	Executive Director, Co-Founder BOFFO
Lloyd Alter	Managing Editor, www.treehugger.com
Kevin Alter	Principal, alterstudio architects and Sid W. Richardson Centennial Professor in Architecture at The University of Texas at Austin
Joseph Altuzarra	Founder, Altuzarra
Amale Andraos	Principal, WORKac and Dean, Columbia University GSAPP
Paola Antonelli	Senior Curator Architecture and Design, MoMA
Michael Arad	Partner, Handel Architects
Ben Aranda	Principal, Aranda\Lasch
Iwan Baan	Principal, Iwan Baan Photography
Spencer Bailey	Editor-in-Chief, Surface Magazine
Matthew Bannister	CEO and Founder, dbox
Ethel Baraona Pohl	Co-Founder, dpr-barcelona
Daniel Barasch	Co-Founder, The Lowline
David Barry	President & CEO, Ironstate Development
Gem Barton	Academic (University of Brighton, UK) and author
Yves Behar	CEO/Chief Designer fuseproject and Co-Founder August
David Benjamin	Principal, The Living
Linda Bennett	Designer and Writer, Founder of architactcollective.com and archininja.com
Dror Benshetrit	Principal, Dror
Barry Bergdoll	Curator, Department of Architecture and Design, The Museum of Modern Art
Kai-Uwe Bergmann	Architect, BIG
Deborah Berke	Deborah Berke Partners
Miljenko Bernfest	Principal, Bernfest Architecture
Fred A. Bernstein	Freelance Architecture Writer and Contributing Editor, Architectural Record and Departures
Charles Bessard	Founding Partner, POWERHOUSE COMPANY
Aaron Betsky	Dean, Frank Lloyd Wright School of Architecture at Taliesin
Charles A. Birnbaum	Founder & President, The Cultural Landscape Foundation
Marlon Blackwell	Principal, Marlon Blackwell Architects
Clément Blanchet	Founding Principal, Clément Blanchet Architecture Professor ESA, Paris Val de Seine, U Michigan
Andrew Blum	Author
Neil Blumenthal	Co-Founder and Co-CEO, Warby Parker
Stefano Boeri	Principal, Stefano Boeri Architetti
Ron Bogle	President and CEO, American Architectural Foundation
Bob Borson	Founder, LifeofanArchitect.com
Ole Bouman	Director of the Shekou Design Museum, Shenzhen
Ronan Bouroullec	Partner, Ronan & Erwan Bouroullec Design
Brian Boylan	Chairman, Wolff Olins
Alan G. Brake	Executive Editor, Architect's Newspaper
Matthew O. Brimer	Founder, General Assembly
Hugh Broughton	Director, Hugh Broughton Architects
Scott Burnham	Urban Strategist, Scott Burnham Studio
Felix Burrichter	Founder, PIN–UP
Collin Burry	Principal, Global Design Leader, Gensler
Casey Caplowe	Co-Founder and Chief Creative Officer, GOOD
John Cary	Founder and Editor, PublicInterestDesign.org
Rachel Casanova	Principal, Director of Workspace Perkins + Will
Charlie Catlett	Director, Urban Center for Computation and Data Senior Computer Scientist, University of Chicago and Argonne National Laboratory
Eric Cesal	Executive Director, Architecture for Humanity
John Cetra	Co-Founder, CetraRuddy
Vishaan Chakrabarti	Principal, SHoP Architects
Tony Chambers	Editor-in-Chief, Wallpaper*
Vikram Chatwal	Founder, Lifestyle Division of Debut Hotels Group
Zohra Chiheb	Architect, Levitt Bernstein
Susan Chin	Executive Director, Design Trust for Public Space

Minsuk Cho	Principal, Mass Studies
Allan Chochinov	Partner, Core77; Chair, SVA MFA Products of Design
Emanuel Christ	Co-Founder, Christ & Gantenbein
Thomas Chung	Associate Professor, School of Architecture, The Chinese University of Hong Kong
Alessandra Cianchetta	Architect & Urban Designer, Founding Partner, AWP Office for territorial reconfiguration
Pippo Ciorra	Senior Curator, MAXXI Architettura
Carter Cleveland	Founder and CEO, Artsy
Brad Cloepfil	Founding Principal, Allied Works Architecture
Andrew B. Cogan	CEO, Knoll
Preston Scott Cohen	Principal, Preston Scott Cohen, Inc.
Chris Colborn	EVP Global Chief Design and Innovation Officer, R/GA
Ian Collings	Co-Founder, Fort Standard
Mickey Conlon	Real Estate Broker and Host of HGTV's Selling New York
Troy Conrad Therrien	Curator, Architecture and Digital Initiatives, Solomon R. Guggenheim Foundation and Museum
Pablo Coppola	Design Director, Bally
James Corner	Founding Partner, James Corner Field Operations
Joseph F. Coughlin	Director, Massachusetts Institute of Technology AgeLab
Carlos Couturier	Co-Founder, Grupo Habita
Isabelle Créach	Marketing Director, Artemide
Ned Cramer	Editor-in-Chief, Architect magazine
Jay Cross	President, Related Hudson Yards
Alan Cumming	Performer
Andreas Dalsgaard	Filmmaker, The Human Scale
Catherine Dannenbring	Director - Sustainability, Skanska Commercial Development
Tom Darden	Executive Director, Make It Right
Justin Davidson	Architecture Critic, New York Magazine
David de Rothschild	Adventurer/Environmentalist
Julien De Smedt	Founder and Director, JDS/JULIEN DE SMEDT ARCHITECTS
Nathalie de Vries	Architect, Urban Planner, and Co-Founder, MVRDV
Jared Della Valle	President, Alloy Development
Nick Denton	Founder, Gawker Media
Herve Descottes	Founder, L'Observatoire International
Alex Diehl	CEO, KKLD*
Liz Diller	Founding Principal, Diller Scofidio + Renfro
Winka Dubbeldam	Principal, ARCHI-TECTONICS Professor and Chair, Department of Architecture, PENNDESIGN, Philadelphia
Roger Duffy	Partner, Skidmore, Owings and Merrill
Cheryl S. Durst	Executive Vice President and CEO, International Interior Design Association/IIDA
Fred Dust	Partner, IDEO
Craig Dykers	Principal, Snøhetta
Mark Dytham	Klein Dytham architecture & PechaKucha Founder
Matias Sendoa Echanove	Co-Founder, Urbanology
John Edelman	CEO, Design Within Reach
William S. Ehrlich	President, Milton L. EHRLICH
Olafur Eliasson	Artist
Gary Elliott	Founding Partner, Elliott Wood Structural and Civil Engineers
Victor Ermoli	Dean, School of Design, SCAD
Peter Espersen	Head of Crowd Sourcing and Online Communities, LEGO
Marcus Fairs	Founder and Editor-in-Chief, Dezeen
Nikolai Fedak	Founder, New York YIMBY
Rick Fedrizzi	President, CEO, and Founding Chair, U.S. Green Building Council
Brad Feinknopf	Architectural Photographer, feinknopf
Nicholas Felton	Founder, Feltron
Sarah Filley	Cofounder and Executive Director, Popuphood CMO, Oppsites
Ben Flanner	Head Farmer, Brooklyn Grange
Nicola Formichetti	Artistic Director, DIESEL

Anne Fougeron	Principal, Fougeron Architecture
Justin Fowler	Founding Editor, Manifest: A Journal of American Architecture and Urbanism
Eva Franch i Gilabert	Executive Director and Chief Curator, Storefront for Art and Architecture
Salomon Frausto	Head of Education, The Berlage Center for Advanced Studies in Architecture and Urban Design
Sou Fujimoto	Principal, Sou Fujimoto Architects
Bruno Gabbiani	President ALA - Assoarchitetti
Pedro Gadanho	Curator, Architecture and Design, MoMA
Beatrice Galilee	Daniel Brodsky Associate Curator of Architecture and Design, The Metropolitan Museum of Art
Jeanne Gang	Principal and Founder, Studio Gang Architects
Christoph Gantenbein	Co-Founder, Christ & Gantenbein
David A. Garcia	Architect MAA, Founder & Director
Joe Gebbia	Co-Founder & CPO, Airbnb
John Gendall	Writer & Critic
Rosalie Genevro	Executive Director, The Architectural League of New York
John Gidding	Founder, Gidding&Spencer, GAVL
MaryAnne Gilmartin	Executive Vice President, Director of Commercial & Residential Development, Forest City Ratner
Marianne Goebl	Managing Director, Artek
Simon Goetz	Partner, Milkshake Studio
Paul Goldberger	Author, Why Architecture Matters
Thelma Golden	Director and Chief Curator, The Studio Museum of Harlem
Wendy Goodman	Design Editor, New York Magazine
Jamie Gray	Founder, Matter
Adam Greenfield	Managing Director, Urbanscale
Joseph Grima	Co-Founder, Space Caviar
Ralf Groene	Sr. Creative Director, Microsoft Surface
Philippe Grohe	Head of Axor, Hansgrohe SE
Rachel Gutter	Senior Vice President of Education, U.S. Green Building Council
Abby Hamlin	President, Hamlin Ventures
Robert Hammond	Co-Founder, Friends of the High Line
Gary Handel	Partner, Handel Architects
Gisue Hariri	Founder & Principal Design Director, Hariri & Hariri - Architecture
Brandon Haw	Senior Partner, Foster + Partners
Christopher Hawthorne	Architecture Critic, LA Times
Jessica Healy	Project Director, USA Pavilion Exp Milano 2015
Kambiz Hemati	Co-Founder, Love Observed Vision Explored
Gunter Henn	Chairman, Henn Architekten
Graham Hill	Founder, LifeEdited and TreeHugger
Cathy Lang Ho	Founder, CLHoffice Commissioner & Lead Curator, U.S. Pavilion, Venice Biennale 2012
Steven Holl	Principal, Steven Holl Architects
Randy J. Hunt	Creative Director, Etsy
Ciel Hunter	Creative Director, The Creators Project
Sarah Ichioka	Director, The Architecture Foundation
Florian Idenburg	Principal, SO – IL
Mirko Ilic	Designer
Jeffrey Inaba	Principal, INABA
Bjarke Ingels	Architect, BIG
Erla Dögg Ingjaldsdóttir	Principal, Minarc
Robert Ivy	Executive Vice President Chief Executive Officer, AIA
Lisa Iwamoto	Partner, IwamotoScott Architecture
Paul J. Lewis	Principal, LTL Architects
Dr. Richard Jackson	Professor of Environmental Health Sciences, UCLA
Sam Jacob	Principal, Sam Jacob Studio for architecture and design
Natasha Jen	Principal, Pentagram

Mark Jensen	Principal, Jensen Architects
Mitchell Joachim	Co-Founder, Terreform ONE
Philip Jodidio	Architecture Editor, Taschen
Casey Jones	Deputy Director, Bureau of Overseas Buildings Operations, U.S. Department of State
Vesna Jovanovic	ETH Studio-Basel
Jiang Jun	Founding Editor in Chief, Urban China Magazine
Anja Kaehny	Director, Espace Louis Vuitton Munich
Julia Kaganskiy	Editor, The Creators Project
Ben Kaufman	Founder, Quirky
Michelle Kaufmann	Principal, Michelle Kaufmann Studio Co-Founder, Flux
Dr. Jesse M. Keenan	Research Director, Center for Urban Real Estate, Columbia University
Paul Kelterborn	Founder, NYC AIDS Memorial Programs Manager, Municipal Art Society
Pat Kiernan	Morning Anchor, NY1 News
Roy Kim	Head of New Development, Compass
Laura Kirar	Founder, Laura Kirar Design
Hubert Klumpner	Dean Architecture Department ETH Zurich, Prof. for Architecture and Urban Design, Co-Founder and Co-Principal of the firm Urban-Think Tan
Tim Kobe	Founder and Principal, Eight Inc.
Aaron Koblin	Co-Founder, CTO - Vrse
Leslie Koch	President, The Trust for Governors Island
Rem D Koolhaas	Founder, United Nude
Amir Korangy	Publisher, The Real Deal
Reed Kroloff	Partner, Jones/Kroloff
Cliff Kuang	Director of Product, Fast Company
Tom Kundig, FAIA	Principal/Owner, Olson Kundig Architects
Mieko Kusano	Senior Director of Design, Sonos
Soon Woo Kwon	Principal, Samoo Architects and Engineers
Chris Lasch	Principal, Aranda\Lasch
Dominic Leong	Partner, Leong Leong
Prof. Dr. Andres Lepik	Direktor Architekturmuseum der Technischen Universität München
David Lewis	Principal, LTL Architects
Ryan Lintott	COO/CTO, Squint Opera
Winy Maas	Architect, Urban Planner, and Co-Founder, MVRDV
Elle Macpherson	Model/Entrepreneur
Eckart Maise	Head of Design and R&D, Vitra
Geoffrey Makstutis	Course Leader, BA (Hons) Architecture: Spaces and Objects, Central Saint Martins/University of the Arts London
Nadav Malin	President, BuildingGreen, Inc.
Jonathan Mallie	Partner, SHoP Architects
Geoff Manaugh	Author, BLDGBLOG
Jennifer Marmon	Founding Partner, Platform for Architecture + Research
Sommer Mathis	Editor, The Atlantic Cities
Juergen Mayer H.	Founding partner, J. Mayer H. and partners
Giancarlo Mazzanti	Architect El Equipo Mazzanti
Rory McGowan	Director, ARUP
Samuel Medina	Associate Editor, Metropolis Magazine
Jeff Miller	VP Product Design, Poppin
Jason Millhouse	Design Manager, The Ritz-Carlton Hotel Company
Marc Mimram	Founding Director, Marc Mimram Architects and Engineers
Josephine Minutillo	Director of Merchandising, Fab.com
Juan Miró	Principal, Miró Rivera Architects
Michael Moran	Principal, Michael Moran Photography
Toshiko Mori	Principal, Toshiko Mori Architect
Eric Owen Moss	Principal, Eric Owen Moss Architects
John Mulling	Design Director, Gensler
Michael Murphy	Founding Partner / Executive Director, MASS Design Group
Alex Mustonen	Co-Founder, Snarkitecture
Alf Naman	Founder, Alf Naman Real Estate Advisors
Daniel Neo Moroka	Board Chairman, Botswana Innovation Hub

Thao Nguyen	Art/Architecture/Design Agent, Creative Artists Agency (CAA)
Philip Nobel	Editorial Director, SHoP
Enrique Norten	Principal, Founder, Ten Arquitectos
Chad Oppenheim	Principal, Oppenheim Architecture + Design LLP
Evan Orensten	Co-Founder, Cool Hunting
Kate Orff	Founder SCAPE / LANDSCAPE ARCHITECTURE. Associate Professor of Architecture and Urban Design, Columbia GSAPP
Laszlo Jakab Orsos	Director, PEN World Voices Festival New York
Shaun Osher	Founder and Chief Executive Officer, CORE
Elisa Ours	Vice President of Planning & Design, Corcoran Sunshine Marketing Group
Christine Outram	Associate Director, Invention	Deutsch LA
Neri Oxman	MIT Media Lab
Gregg Pasquarelli	Principal, SHoP Architects
Deborah Patton	Executive Director, Applied Brilliance
Chee Pearlman	Editorial and Curatorial Projects, Chee Company Inc.
Shelley Penn	Architect. Past National President, Australian Institute of Architects
Lisa Phiilips	Director, New Museum
Lisa Picard	Executive Vice President, Skanska USA Commercial Development
Sara Polsky	Senior Features Editor, Curbed
Ernest Pomerantz	Managing Director, StoneWater Capital LLC
Monica Ponce de Leon	Dean and Eliel Saarinen Collegiate Professor, Taubman College of Architecture and Urban Planning, University of Michigan	President, Monica Ponce de Leon Studio
Tom Postilio	Real Estate Broker and Host of HGTV's Selling New York
Joshua Prince-Ramus	Principal, REX
Benjamin Prosky	Assistant Dean for Communications, Harvard Graduate School of Design
James Ramsey	Co-Founder, The Lowline Principal, RAAD
Rankin	Photographer and Director, Rankin Photography
Guy Raz	Host, TED Radio Hour NPR
Elias Redstone	Curator
Charles Renfro	Principal, Diller Scofidio + Renfro
Heinz Richardson	Director, Jestico + Whiles
Alan Ricks	Co-Founder, MASS Design Group
Anne Rieselbach	Program Director, The Architectural League NY
Terence Riley	Principal, K/R
Mark Robbins	Executive Director, International Center of Photography
Craig Robins	CEO and President, Dacra
David Rockwell	Principal, David Rockwell Group
Roo Rogers	Partner, fuseproject
Fernando Romero	Founder, FREE
Kimerly Rorschach	Illsley Ball Nordstrom Director and CEO, Seattle Art Museum
Cynthia Rowley	Founder, Cynthia Rowley
Josh Rubin	Founder and Editor in Chief, Cool Hunting
Arthur Rubinfeld	Chief Creative Officer and President, Global Development and Evolution Fresh Retail, Starbucks Coffee Company
Dan Rubinstein	Home + Design Editor, Departures
Matthias Rudolph	Climate Engineer, Transsolar / Professor of building technology and climate design, Stuttgart State Academy of Art and Design, Germany
James S. Russell	Freelance Critic and Journalist
Joel Sanders	Principal, JSA
Ian Schrager	Founder and Chairman, Ian Schrager Company
Craig Schwitter	Principal, Buro Happold Consulting Engineers
Craig Scott	Partner, IwamotoScott Architecture
Susanne Seitinger	Senior Technologist, Philips Color Kinetics
Tim Seldin	President, The Montessori Foundation
Evan Sharp	Co-Founder, Pinterest
Christopher Sharples	Partner, SHoP Architects
Andrew Shea	Principal, MANY Design	Author, Designing for Social Change	Visiting Professor, Parsons the New School for Design and Pratt Institute
Rachel Shechtman	Founder, Story
Shohei Shigamatsu	Partner, OMA

Michael Shvo	President and CEO, SHVO
Jason Silva	Filmmaker
Cameron Sinclair	Founder, Department of Small Works
Jonathan D. Solomon	Director of Architecture, Interior Architecture and Designed Objects, School of the Art Institute of Chicago
Nancy Spector	Deputy Director and Jennifer and David Stockman Chief Curator, Solomon R. Guggenheim Foundation
Morgan Spurlock	Filmmaker
Rahul Srivastava	Founder, Urbanology
Lockhart Steele	Founder, Curbed
Michael Stern	Founder, JDS Development Group
Claudia Strauss	CEO, Grey Activation & PR
Yancey Strickler	CEO and Co-Founder, Kickstarter
John A. Stuart	Professor and Associate Dean for Cultural and Community Engagement, FIU College of Architecture + The Arts
Terrie Sultan	Director, Parrish Art Museum
John M. Syvertsen	Chair, Board of Regents, American Architectural Foundation
Dr. Angelika Taschen	Publisher
Sue Tatge	VP, Director of Media, Wray Ward
Piers Taylor	Architect, Principal of Invisible Studio
Marilyn Taylor	Dean and Paley Professor, School of DesignUniversity of Pennsylvania
Christopher Tepper	Founder, NYC AIDS Memorial
Ghana ThinkTank	John Ewing, Maria del Carmen Montoya and Christoper Robbins
Tryggvi Thorsteinsson	Principal, Minarc
Olivier Touraine	Architect DPLG. Assoc. AIA
Anthony Townsend	Senior Research Fellow, NYU Rudin Center for Transportation
Marc Tsurumaki	Principal, LTL Architects
Gregory Tuck	Director Coach International Architecture, Coach Inc.
Adam Reed Tucker	Founder, Brickstructures, Inc.

Hunter Tura	President and CEO, Bruce Mau Design, Inc.
Henry Urbach	Director, The Glass House
Carolina Vaccaro	Principal, Architect and Design Professor Temple University Rome Campus
Ben van Berkel	Founder/Principal Architect UNStudio
David van der Leer	Executive Director, Van Alen Institute
Jacob van Rijs	Architect, Urbanist, and Co-Founder MVRDV
John Varvatos	Chairman / Founder / Designer
Laurent Vernhes	Co-Founder and CEO, TabletHotels.com
Neil Vogel	CEO, About.com
David Von Spreckelsen	President, Toll Brothers City Living in New York City
Mieke Vullings	Co-Founder & Executive Director, MIMOA
Seth Weisman	Founder, Weissman Equities
Robert Wennett	President, UIA Management
Gregory Wessner	Executive Director, Open House New York
Lynda Whittle	Vice President of Marketing, Allsteel
Gina B. Wicker	Creative Director, Glen Raven Inc, makers of Sunbrella
Elvia Wilk	Freelance Writer, Contributing Editor at uncube magazine
Chris Wilkinson	Founding Director, Wilkinson Eyre Architects
Adam Wilson	Assistant Professor, School of Technology and Design, New York City College of Technology
Max Wolff	Director of Design, Lincoln
Karen Wong	Deputy Director, New Museum
Dan Wood	Principal, WORKac
Ma Yansong	Founding Principal, MAD Architects
Andrew Zobler	Founder and CEO, Sydell Group Ltd.
Andrew Zolli	Executive Director, PopTech
Andrew Zolty	Co-Founder and Chief Creative Officer, BREAKFAST
Andrew Zuckerman	Founder, Andrew Zuckerman Studio

Product Winners Jury

Category	Furniture: Seating - Contract
Title	Rox
Manufacturer	Davis Furniture
	www.davisfurniture.com
	Offered as a rocker or a fixed-base chair, Rox will be an exciting addition to any office, lobby, or collaborative area.

Category	Accessories: Accessories - All
Title	Lap(r)is
Manufacturer	Van den Weghe
	www.vandenweghe.be
	Lap(r)is are in marble integrated plug-sockets.

Category	Plumbing: Kitchen - Fixtures & Fittings
Title	KWC ONO touch light PRO
Manufacturer	KWC America
	www.kwcamerica.com
	The KWC ONO touch light PRO is a kitchen faucet that allows for wireless control of water flow and temperature.

Category	Furniture: Furniture - Contract
Title	BuzziPicNic
Manufacturer	BuzziSpace
	www.buzzispace.com
	An Indoor Picnic Table and Bench System from BuzziSpace provides the perfect option for any office.

Category	Materials: Stone & Concrete
Title	Earth Blox
Manufacturer	Tangrungcharoen Factory, Thailand
	www.sansiri.com
	Recycle concrete blocks from lightweight concrete wasted material at construction sites.

Category	Lighting: Decorative Lighting
Title	VESSEL by 3M™ + Todd Bracher
Manufacturer	3M Architectural Markets
	www.3m.com
	VESSEL by 3M™ + Todd Bracher is perfectly calibrated to eliminate glare and cast a gorgeous light.

Category	Building Products: Building Products
Title	Lamberts Channel Glass Wall Systems
Manufacturer	Bendheim Wall Systems Inc.
	www.bendheim.com
	Lamberts channel glass systems create sweeping glass walls without intermediate framing.

Category	Plumbing: Bath - Cabinetry
Title	M-Series Cabinets
Manufacturer	Robern
	www.us.kohler.com
	M-Series cabinets boast customizable features to provide the ultimate in design and function.

Category	Materials: Textiles
Title	Biobased Xorel
Manufacturer	Carnegie
	www.carnegiefabrics.com
	Biobased Xorel is the world's first high-performance interior textile with a majority of plant-based content.

Category	Lighting: Architectural Lighting
Title	SunBeamer 500
Manufacturer	SunCentral
	www.suncentralinc.com
	The SunBeamer 500 uses optical components to redirect sunlight into building interiors.

Category	Furniture: Residential
Title	Riveli Shelving System
Manufacturer	Lake and Wells
	www.lakeandwells.com
	Riveli is a modular, patented shelving system comprised of individually-pivoting shelves.

Category	Building Products: Windows
Title	Zola No Compromise (ZNC)
Manufacturer	Zola Windows
	www.zolawindows.com
	Uncompromising projects require an uncompromising window with outstanding thermal performance.

Category	Equipment: Appliances
Title	4K Ultra Short Throw Projector
Manufacturer	Sony Corporation
	www.sony.net
	This cutting-edge projector redefines the living space as an immersive user experience.

Category	Plumbing: Kitchen - Cabinetry
Title	Phoenix Kitchen
Manufacturer	Varenna by Poliform
	www.poliformusa.com
	Phoenix is a modular kitchen system distinguished by subtle and pure geometric lines.

Category	Finishes: Flooring - Soft
Title	Neva Fade
Manufacturer	TSAR Carpets
	www.tsarcarpets.com
	An innovation in the classic cut-and-loop pile technique allows for gradation in wool and silk.

Category	Furniture: Furniture - Outdoor
Title	Finn Outdoor Collection
Manufacturer	Design Within Reach
	www.dwr.com
	Designed by Norm Architects, the Finn Collection combines utility, purity, and quiet beauty.

Category	Building Products: Facades
Title	Facade Innovations with Ultra High Performance Concrete
Manufacturer	TAKTL
	www.taktl-llc.com
	TAKTL's technical and aesthetic innovations offer new possibilities for facade design and performance.

Category	Finishes: Flooring - HardVESSEL by 3M™ + Todd Bracher
Title	EDGE
Manufacturer	Fireclay Tile
	www.fireclaytile.com
	A large-format tile with precision cut edges available in three sizes, including the largest tile size on the market.

Category	Materials: Glass
Title	CRT Glass Tile
Manufacturer	Fireclay Tile
	www.fireclaytile.com
	CRT Tile is handmade from 100% post-consumer e-waste.

Category	Building Products: Hardware
Title	Swivel Ceiling Hook
Manufacturer	Hangman Products
	www.linetolinedesign.com
	A sharp-looking swivel ceiling hook provides safe and easy installation for supporting heavy loads.

Category	Finishes: Ceilings
Title	BASWA cool
Manufacturer	BASWA acoustic
	www.baswaphon.com
	Seamless design coupled with radiant cooling and extremely efficient sound absorption.

Category	Plumbing: Bath - Fixtures & Fittings
Title	WallDrain
Manufacturer	QuickDrain USA
	www.quickdrainusa.com
	Vertical shower drain with unlimited design options. A revolution in shower design.

Category	Finishes: Wall Coverings
Title	The Reveal Collection
Manufacturer	Smith & Fong Co. Plyboo
	www.plyboo.com
	The Reveal collection is a series of carved and textured bamboo panels, manufactured by Plyboo.

Category	Building Products: Access
Title	System 1000
Manufacturer	astec
	www.astec-design.ca
	High-performance floor bearing system for sliding panels of ANY size or weight.

Category	Lighting: Lighting Accessories
Title	Solarpuff
Manufacturer	Solight Design
	www.solight-design.com
	The Solar Inflatable Light enables community gatherings in rural areas and provides safety after disaster.

Product Winners Popular Choice

Category	Plumbing: Kitchen - Cabinetry
Title	The Cut Kitchen
Manufacturer	Record è Cucine

www.alessandroisola.com
The Cut reconfigures the kitchen as a space for congregation, relaxation and dining.

Category	Plumbing: Kitchen - Fixtures & Fittings
Title	JUSTIME LUCKY 7 Water Drinking Faucet
Manufacturer	Sheng Tai Brassware Co.

www.justime.com
The Lucky 7 water drinking faucet is the perfect harmony between technology, design and ecology.

Category	Product Categories	Furniture: Furniture - Residential
Title	tension-compression table
Manufacturer	silva aedes

www.silvaaedes.com
Steel and glass tables inspired by bridge design and anthropomorphic mechanics.

Category	Finishes: Ceilings
Title	Revelation SkyCeiling Virtual Skylight
Manufacturer	The Sky Factory

www.skyfactory.com
An illusory sky designed for the larger, higher ceilings common in commercial architecture.

Category	Furniture: Seating - Contract
Title	Mimeo™
Manufacturer	Allsteel

www.allsteeloffice.com
Mimeo supports the changing workplace by enabling unrestricted movement throughout the day.

Category	Materials: Glass
Title	Laser Cut Textiles in Poured Glass
Manufacturer	Studio by 3form

www.3-form.com
Poured Glass features suspended, flowing laser cut textiles for added depth and detail.

Category	Furniture: Furniture - Outdoor
Title	CIRCUIT Lounge
Manufacturer	TJOKEEFE

www.tjokeefe.com
Powder-coated bent steel rod lounge chair suitable for indoor or outdoor use.

Category	Lighting: Lighting Accessories
Title	The Edison Cloud
Manufacturer	Jen Lewin Studio

www.jenlewinstudio.com
The Edison Cloud is a series of 5 chandeliers that create an interactive lighting element.

Category	Lighting: Architectural Lighting
Title	String Lights
Manufacturer	FLOS

www.usa.flos.com
String Lights can be stretched and pinned to create 3D lines and forms.

Category	Building Products: Hardware
Title	Schlage® NDE Series wireless lock with ENGAGE™ technology
Manufacturer	Allegion

www.allegionengage.com
The Schlage® NDE Series wireless lock is designed to be easy to install, connect, and manage.

Category	Furniture: Furniture - Contract
Title	WEB Partition System
Manufacturer	LOFTwall

www.LOFTwall.com
WEB is a freestanding partition designed as a visual barrier to provide privacy and light.

Category	Flooring - Hard
Title	Urban_Avenue
Manufacturer	Ceramica Fioranese

www.fioranese.it
URBAN_AVENUE is porcelain stoneware with the look of bricks for an industrial air.

Category	Materials: Stone & Concrete
Title	Materials, Metal & Stone
Manufacturer	Apotex Aluminum Composite Panel & Kalesinterflex (thin Ceramic tile) Provenza Stone (digital porcelain) Italgranite Stone Mix (high tech porcelain) www.kneiderarchitects.com Materials, Metal & Stone by TTMAC combines new and innovative products from Canada & Europe.

Category	Building Products: Access
Title	MIMO
Manufacturer	Muraflex www.muraflex.com Muraflex is a flexible, demountable partition that allows for quick floorplan changes.

Category	Building Products: Windows
Title	FoldUp™ Window
Manufacturer	HeartWood Fine Windows and Doors www.heartwoodwindows anddoors.com FoldUp™ has the appearance of a double hung window but easily folds up vertically.

Category	Building Products: Facades
Title	Bios self-cleaning
Manufacturer	Casalgrande Padana www.casalgrandepadana.com Self-cleaning ceramic for exterior facades that reduce the airborne pollutants.

Category	Accessories: Accessories - All
Title	F.Domes - Self Assembly Geodesic Dome Kits
Manufacturer	Freedomes www.fdomes.com F.Domes Kits are ready-to-assemble geodesic domes that can be easily turned into multiuse spaces.

Category	Finishes: Flooring - Soft
Title	The Studio/Painting
Manufacturer	Shaw Hospitality Group www.shawinc.com A collaboration with Farmboy Fine Arts, exploring the process of an artist mastering a single work.

Category	Building Products: Building Products
Title	ORIGAMI
Manufacturer	Marretti Stairs www.marretti.com A staircase made from CORTEN, featuring a unique design with an ultrathin thickness of 8 mm.

Category	Materials: Textiles
Title	GreenScreen® Evolve™
Manufacturer	Mermet www.hunterdouglascontract.com 100% recyclable, zero-waste, shade fabric made from post-industrial and post-consumer waste.

Category	Plumbing: Bath - Cabinetry
Title	SUEN (Tenon)
Manufacturer	Taipei Base Design Center www.asia-bdc.com SUEN comes from the Chinese pronunciation of Tenon.

Category	Lighting: Decorative Lighting
Title	Induction Tube Light
Manufacturer	Castor Design www.castordesign.ca Then Induction Tube Light uses a magnetic field to transfer current from its base to a fluorescent bulb.

Category	Finishes: Wall Coverings
Title	Wabi 'River'
Manufacturer	Calico Wallpaper www.calicowallpaper.com River is inspired by the landscapes of the ancient east, invoking the quality of water flowing over stone.

Category	Equipment: Appliances
Title	4K Ultra Short Throw Projector
Manufacturer	Sony Corporation www.sony.net This cutting-edge projector redefines the living space as an immersive user experience.

Category	Plumbing: Bath - Fixtures & Fittings
Title	WallDrain
Manufacturer	QuickDrain USA www.quickdrainusa.com Vertical shower drain with unlimited design options. Not an evolution but a revolution in shower design.

Index

Acknowledgements

This book is dedicated to the world's architects.

Thanks to the Architizer team, with a special thanks to Catherine Finsness, Nikki-Lee Birdsay, and Luna Bernfest.

Phaidon Press Limited
Regent's Wharf
All Saints Street
London N1 9PA

Phaidon Press Inc.
65 Bleecker Street
New York, NY 10012

www.phaidon.com

First published 2015
© 2015 Phaidon Press Limited

ISBN 978 0 7148 7054 0

A CIP catalogue record for this book is available from the British Library and the Library of Congress.

Commissioning Editor: Emilia Terragni
Project Editor: Laura Loesch-Quintin
Production Controllers: Nerissa Vales, Sue Medlicott
Design: Aaron Garza

Printed in U.S.A.

Photography Credits

Scott Adams: pp196–197; Aeroview: pp34–35; Anotherstudio: pp162–163; Takeshi Asano: pp74–75; Emile Ashley: pp34–35; Iwan Baan: pp50–51, 66–67, 98–99, 102–103, 130–131; Matthew Bannister/DBOX: pp38–39; Amy Barkow: pp202–203; Richard Barnes: pp156–157; Bedrock Real Estate Service: pp150–15; Belzberg Architects: pp42–43; David Benjamin: pp102–103; Team BIG: pp136–137; Jeremy Bittermann: pp160–161; BMW China: pp158–159; Brett Boardman: pp58–59; Scott Bonney, AIA: pp150–151; Kritsada Boonchaleaw: pp46–47; Jomar Bragança: pp146–147; Marcus Buck: pp124–125; Tamás Bujnovszky: pp170–171; Calder Foundation Project Space: pp96–97; Jose Campos Architectural Photography: pp116–117; Benny Chan: pp42–43; Christian Richters: pp182–183, 98–99; Bieke Claessens: pp124–125; Ryan Clark: pp186–187; Bruce Damonte: pp42–43; De Leon & Primmer Architecture Workshop: pp56–57; Tim Van De Velde: pp174–175; Decopic: pp188–189; Alex DeRijke: pp34–35; DISSING+WEITLING architecture: pp152–153; Studio Dubuisson: pp52–53; Filip Dujardin: pp124–125; Casey Dunn: pp198–199; Sindre Ellingsen: pp34–35; Bruce Engel: pp166–167; Esto: pp184–185; James Ewing: pp50–51; Raphael Faux: pp98–99; Elizabeth Felicella: pp166–167; Leonardo Finotti: pp24–25; Jake Fitzjones: pp20–21; Joe Fletcher: pp142–143; Joana França: pp126–127; Jonathan Friedman/Partisans: pp80–81; Karen Fuchs: pp38–39; Rafael Gamo: pp180–181; Philippe Van Gelooven: pp124–125; GLUCK+: pp202–203; Jeff Goldberg/Esto: pp122–123; Adam Goss: pp186–187; Tim Griffith: pp48–49; Simon Grimes: pp58–59; Fernando Guerra, FG+SG: pp26–27; Roland Halbe: pp100–101; Steve Hall, Hedrich Blessing: pp86–87; Mike Dugenio Hansen: pp152–153; Luke Hayes: pp78–79; Sean Hemmerle: pp164–165; Edward Hendricks: pp54–55; Hannes Henz: pp30–31; Mark Herboth Photography: pp122–123; John Horner: pp118–119; Charles Hosea: pp10–11; Mika Huisman: pp188–189; Hundven-Clements Photography: pp108–109; Greg Irikura: pp204–205; Krista Jahnke: pp104–105; Miran Kambič: pp148–149; J. Kane-Hartnett: pp164–165; Yusuke Kataoka: pp110–111; Donát Kékesi: pp170–171; Yongkwan Kim: pp84–85; Cam Koroluk: pp104–105; Thomas Kosbau: pp134–135; Naho Kubota: pp204–205; Kevin Kunstadt: pp94–95; Robert Lemermeyer: pp168–169; Jens Lindhe: pp90–91; Francesco Lipari: pp162–163; David Duncan Livingston: pp206–207; Maisam Architects & Engineers: pp138–139; Ole Malling: pp152–153; Nick Merrick: pp200–201; Red Mike: pp186–187; Saša Miljevi c: pp172–173; Millimeter Interior Design: pp174–175; João Morgado: pp192–193; Adam Mørk: pp92–93; Jaime Navarro: pp120–121; Mike Neale: pp10–11; Neumann/Smith Architecture: pp150–151; Mikael Olsson: pp82–83; Chad Oppenheim: pp38–39; Fernando Ortega: pp196–197; PARA: pp16–17; Pedro Pegenaute: pp62–63; Time Street Porter: pp128–129; People's Architecture Office: pp178–179; Pierer.net: pp72–73; Robert Polidori: pp140–141; Joakim Lloyd Raboff: pp128–129; Tihomir Rachev: pp76–77; Rasmus Hjortshøj-Coast Studio: pp152–153; Rebuild by Design: pp194–195; Tuca Reines: pp24–25; Reiulf Ramstad Architects: pp108–109; Christian Richters: pp98–99; Paul Riddle: pp20–21; Laura Torres Roa: pp112–113; Charles Roussel: pp102–103; Yohei Sasakura: pp176–177; Sergio Saucedo: pp134–135; Martin Schubert: pp90–91; Goran Šebelić: pp172–173; Javier Callejas Sevilla: pp44–45; Shengliang: pp114–115; Kyungsub Shin: pp68–69, 84–85; Eric Sierins: pp96–97, 32–33; Toshihiro Sobajima: pp14–15; Ansis Starks: pp28–29; Studio Farris Architects: pp36–37; Parham Taghioff: pp70–71; Géza Talabér: pp170–171; Ruy Teixeira: pp24–25; Svetoslav Todorov: pp76–77; Ka-Man Tse: pp164–165; Yen-Chih Tseng: pp60–61; Wison Tungthunya: pp46–47; Sandy Wang: pp104–105; Paul Warchol: pp22–23; Kikuma Watanaeb: pp110–111; Craig Van Wieren of Modern Edge Studios: pp150–151; Michele Lee Willson Photography: pp132–133; Patrick Winn: pp196–197; Jan Kofod Winther: pp90–91; Yu Xu: pp114–115; Xia Zhi: pp12–13.